July 4, 1776

The dramatic story of the
first four days of July, 1776

By DONALD BARR CHIDSEY

Wildside Press

TO JOAN CLARK CHIDSEY

Contents

On Looking Up	1
Part One: *July 1*	3
Part Two: *July 2*	53
Part Three: *July 3*	71
Part Four: *July 4*	87
Part Five: *Afterward*	97
Notes	128
Appendix	138
Index	149

On Looking Up

WHEN one stares up at this group of Fathers, these illustrious statesmen, one has an urge to behave like a boy with a snowball who is confronted with a whole covey of high silk hats. One twitches.

Is not debunking an applauded pastime? Would not cheers arise, howsoever poor the aim, for haven't we all had the paragons pointed out to us too many times by over-rapturous schoolmarms? Wouldn't everyone rather have an ideal *shown* up than *held* up?

The temptation must be stifled. All rodomontade aside, these were great men. True, they tended to wax polysyllabic, but on the whole they remained at least grammatical; sometimes they rose to heights of eloquence; and in any event, is pomposity, then, lacking in our current halls of legislature? Of course the Signers took themselves seriously! They were attending at the birth of a nation, a serious duty. Those pedestals were not their familiar, accustomed standing places, but rather columns propped underneath them when the Signers no longer could resist, being dead. We should regard, then, not the marble, the stone phrases ("In lapidary inscriptions a man is not upon oath"—Johnson), but rather the flesh above. It is found to be human.

Part One: *July 1*

IT WOULD BE a hot day. Already, at six o'clock, it was sticky, and what wind there was was from the south. These details were jotted down by a tall, red-haired young Virginian who had rented two rooms on the second floor of a new red-brick house at the southwest corner of Market and Seventh streets, Philadelphia.[1] A painstaking diarist, he also made note of the fact that he distrusted his thermometer and meant to get a new one at the earliest opportunity. Then, having finished his breakfast, Thomas Jefferson set forth for a committee meeting.

He was a methodical man, and it is not likely that his step this morning was faster or slower than usual; but his heart must have been beating thirteen to the dozen, for this was the day when the independence resolutions would come up on the floor of the Continental Congress, the day for crossing or refusing to cross the Rubicon.

Six A.M. was not an exceptional hour for a delegate to be going to work. If anything, it was late. Throughout most of the year the sessions, six a week, starting at ten o'clock, continued without break until three or four, dinner-time. A little while ago the starting hour had been advanced to nine o'clock. This left only the evening and early morning for committee work; and there was a great deal of committee work, necessarily, for the Congress, a body unrecognized by any government on earth —or even by most of the people in the thirteen American colonies it pretended to rule—without any previous experience, but earnestly, had taken upon itself the task of building an army and a navy, waging war against the greatest power in the world, arranging for supplies, establishing factories, locating and working mines, imposing taxes upon men who had not authorized them, hatching out thirteen separate colonial eggs and motherhenning them when hatched, printing money, appointing

Thomas Jefferson, *painted in 1786 by Mather Brown. Courtesy Mr. Charles Francis Adams and Colonial Williamsburg.*

ambassadors, and otherwise governing two and a half million persons, not including Indians. More than half a million of these were Negroes. Also, this population was increasing, and at an amazing rate. Men were marrying early, and widows didn't remain widows very long. It was estimated that the number of persons in the colonies was doubling itself every twenty to twenty-five years, a statistic that the English ministers must have taken into anxious consideration in the course of the long transoceanic disagreement that seemed now at last to be reaching a climax, a figure the go-slow men in Congress were wont to hold up as an additional reason for moderation, delay. This population was not clumped. Mr. Jefferson's own Virginia, though it had no city and its Williamsburg was called "that toy capital," was easily the largest with 504,264, Massachusetts with 290,000 being second. Then came, close together, Pennsylvania, Maryland, North Carolina, and Connecticut. New York was seventh,[2] Georgia last. North of the Mason-Dixon line there were 1,298,763 residents, among them 57,000 slaves; south of that line there were 1,208,417, Negro slaves accounting for 482,700 of these.

Here was a great responsibility, as the Congress knew. It was not uncommon to have committee meetings before breakfast. Almost certainly there were at least a few in progress even while Mr. Jefferson left the home of Frederic Graaf, that recently married young bricklayer, an immigrant.

But wherever they were, the fifty-odd members of the Congress that morning in Philadelphia were thinking of one thing and one thing only—independence.

A little while ago the very word had been anathema. It had been spoken, and more than once, in both houses of Parliament, where the possibility that the American colonies might set up a republic was faced; but in the colonies themselves, until the other day, it had been repudiated with a stress all but hysterical.

Richard Penn, questioned in the House of Lords, averred that he had "never heard one of them [the colonists] breathe sentiments of that nature," and shortly before Benjamin Franklin left England he had told Lord Chatham that "having more than once travelled almost from one end of the continent to the other and kept a great variety of company, eating, drinking, and conversing with them freely, I [have] never heard in any conversation, from any person drunk or sober, the least expression of a wish for a separation or hint that such a thing would be advantageous to America." Washington, on his way to take command of the Continental Army, had roundly declared that he "abhorred" the idea of independence—though he had since then changed his mind. The sarcastic Carter Braxton of Virginia, who had taken his seat only last February, esteemed independence "in truth a delusive bait which men inconsiderately catch at, without knowing the hook to which it is affixed." The month before, on the advice of the Continental Congress, the provincial committee of New Hampshire had adopted a constitution specifically designed to last "only during the present unhappy and unnatural contest with Great Britain." That same month—on January 6, 1776, to be exact—the Continental Congress itself had adopted a resolution protesting that it had "no design to set up as an independent nation."

None of this did the English statesmen, cynical chaps, believe; yet it was true. Hundreds of similar instances could be cited. The American colonies, ever since the first stirrings of misunderstanding with the mother country, in 1763, had so disliked the concept of independence that they didn't even want to talk about it. It was the ministers in England who had insisted that a desire for separation was the only conceivable explanation of the way the colonists were acting. Colonial protestations of devotion, of sincerity, were of course absurd; they could only be hypocritical. You don't love a man and shoot at him, do you? So often and with such intensity did the English make this point that after a while the colonists, tired, began, a few at a time, to agree. Once started, the movement grew rapidly. You were not obliged to whisper when you spoke the word "independence" now. There were even whose who shouted it. And assuredly it would be shouted again, soon, this very morning, when the delegates to the Second Continental Congress foregathered at the State House.

Old State House, Philadelphia. *Engraving by J. Rogers.*

This building was perhaps the most famous and surely one of the handsomest in the land.³ The Congressmen had been assigned to a fine chamber on the ground floor, the Pennsylvania Assembly amiably moving upstairs to make room for them. They had the center of the building, then, pretty much to themselves; for the Assembly, in trouble, racked by radicals, was "in a state of masterly inactivity," and as often as not didn't meet at all. The west wing was occupied, downstairs, by the doorkeeper of the Assembly and his family; the east wing, upstairs, by visiting Indians, whose carelessness with fire greatly perturbed the doorkeeper at the other end, for, though the building was made of brick, there were sundry wooden sheds near the wall, and those were very flammable indeed.

* * * * *

Regard these delegates to the Second Continental Congress as they converge here. They are sober men, carefully dressed. There are no Marats among them, no Kropotkins or Lenins. So far from being hot-eyed fanatics yammering for an explosion, they have but asked, in a dignified if dogged manner, for a return to the *status quo ante*. Change they do not seek, but resist. It is King George and his myopic ministers who would impose change upon them. It is from across the sea that the wild governmental proposals have been coming ever since the close of the French and Indian War, the taking-over of Canada, thirteen years ago—a proposal to enforce the laws against smuggling, a proposal to decree that royal governors shall be paid a set sum by the colonies they govern, proposals to tax legal papers, paint, playing cards. How can a man make money, in a community dependent upon the outside world for all its manufactured goods, if he has to go through customs? Smuggling had been good enough for our mercantile forebears: Why shouldn't it be good enough for us? How can you induce a royal governor to sign something obnoxious to him unless you threaten to withhold his pay? As for taxes, not only were they pestiferous, and clearly illegal; they constituted a perilous precedent. Who knew where taxation, given its head, might stop? It wasn't the money, it was the principle of the thing— a fact that the arrogant ones in England simply refused to grasp. For example, after most of the Townshend Acts had been repealed, following the repeal of the Stamp Act, after glass and paint and paper had been granted free access into the colonies, only tea was left. But the tax on tea, in the colonies, was to be but threepence a pound, and at the same time the bill provided for the repeal of the export tax of one shilling a pound in England, a charge inevitably passed on to the consumer. In other words, the law would have made tea *cheaper* for the Americans.

This had been done not out of charity but in the hope of counteracting the trade in contraband, untaxed tea from Holland. Yet the colonists, those fools, objected! The tea tax was trifling—or would have been. Plans were to raise a mere £16,000 a year on it, from all thirteen colonies. Yet the mad Americans—to mention but one instance—had hurled tea valued at £18,000 into Boston harbor when they could not arrange to have it shipped back in protest; and despite all threats to their commerce they refused even to discuss the possibility of compensation.[4] What was more, the other ports, which might have profited from the ruination of Boston when that port in punishment was closed down, had stood behind Boston! From being puzzled, and baffled, Whitehall had become angry. The voice of the court was strident now.

Regard then these men who file into the State House. *They* could have explained, and repeatedly they had tried to explain. The tea tax might have meant a lower price immediately, yes; but it would have been a foot in the doorway, the camel's nose inside the tent.

They knew what resistance might cost, these conservatives. They could count. Many were successful merchants, who could calculate the cost of a war as of a keg of nails. More than half were lawyers. All were propertied men, responsible men, and not a few of them rich.

Was there still time to turn back? Or should they say, today, after Caesar, *Jacta alea est*—the die is cast?

True, there was talk that the throne had named peace commissioners who were already on their way to America, but nobody took much stock in this. The rulers in London had been wont to hold out now a sword, now an olive branch, alternating these so swiftly sometimes that they seemed to be holding both at once. But this time, assuredly, it was the sword; and whatever talk of peace commissioners there might be was cover-up. However, it could prove embarrassing, in that it gave the die-hards some slight additional ammunition. The cry rose once again: Let's not hurry into anything! At the same time, the talk of peace commissioners toughened the independence men. General Washington had written from the field as early as March 24 asking Congress what he should do if peace commissioners landed in Boston, a city he had just taken. The answer, not framed until May 6, had been:

> Resolved, That General Washington be informed, that the Congress suppose, if commissioners are intended to be sent from Great Britain to treat of peace, that the practice usual in such cases will be observed, by making previous application for the necessary passports or safe conduct, and on such application being made, Congress will then direct the proper measures for the reception of such commissioners.

That is: we will cross this bridge when we come to it, if we ever do. The Second Continental Congress, an utterly illegal body, lacked precedent in this as in so many other matters; but it did not lack aplomb.

Smaller groups were less wary. On April 6 the South Carolina convention resolved that any such commissioners should be sent back within forty-eight hours of their arrival, "wind and weather permitting," and meanwhile held incommunicado, *unless* they bore credentials addressed to the Continental Congress, thereby accepting the same as a legal entity. Six days later the provincial congress of North Carolina, a colony until then believed to have a high proportion of Tories—or as they preferred to call themselves, loyalists—had come out formally for independence, so instructing its delegates to the Continental Congress. And the day after that, April 13, this same assembly had passed a resolution declaring that "unless such commissioner or commissioners shall produce a commission to treat with the Continental Congress, he or they should be required to return immediately on board the vessel in which he or they arrived." If the entrance had been made by land, then he or they should be conducted right back over the border.

So much for the olive branch, which, waved, was to prove a brittle reed. The sword was something else.

Howe had evacuated Boston in March, making for Halifax. Now he was back, as expected, off New York, but back in much

July 4, 1776

greater strength, his ranks having been swollen by Cossacks from the Russian steppes or, some said, Dutchmen or Germans, barbarians anyway, thugs who would be quick to rape, loot, burn.

The news had reached Philadelphia that very morning, Monday, July 1, 1776. Only two days before, the first of Howe's sails had been sighted off Sandy Hook, and now they covered the ocean, the most stupendous flotilla any man ever had seen, bigger even than the Spanish Armada.

The men who must decide how to meet this invasion were assembling again in Philadelphia. It was a time of bright clothing, a peacock age, but these delegates were somberly clad. It was a sunshiny morning, but they were staid, weighed down by responsibility. They were not revolutionists—they thought themselves the very opposite—and any one of them might have summoned you to the field of honor, or at least threatened to do so, if you called him a rebel, a word that could make any of them wince.

They bowed to one another when they met—those who were still on speaking terms—for although the debate might be bitter, the bitterest yet, as they faced, having at last to face, the inescapable issue, yet they must keep up appearances. On paper there never was a dissenting voice in the Continental Congress. The first such body, two years ago, had established this as a precedent. Unanimity they could not hope for and perhaps never had aspired to, but a show of unity might be all that kept them and their ideals alive. Each was pledged not to divulge the doings on the floor, which from time to time were sufficiently furious. Fists might be shaken, voices raised, and they were, but no news of this, it was fondly hoped, would seep into the world outside. Visitors never were admitted. Proceedings never were published, or even recorded in any detail. "The child Independence is now struggling for birth," Samuel Adams had written a friend a few months ago. "I trust that in a short time it will be brought forth and in spite of Pharaoh all America shall hail the dignified stranger." If Independence was in truth a babe, and if it was to be born, here, this day, or the next day, or the next, there would be no immediate fanfare. Rather would it be *sneaked* into the world, its existence not announced until the Fathers, those cautious men, had determined that it was not a miscarriage—or a monster.

Already, indoors, the clerk of the Congress, Charles Thompson, an adroit municipal organizer, "the Samuel Adams of Philadelphia," a classical scholar who to take this exacting job had interrupted his life work of translating the Bible from its original tongues, though he didn't need the money, having just made a rich marriage, his second—already the clerk, at a desk appropriately placed a little to the left, was shuffling his papers, clearing his throat, opening letters, jotting down reminders. He did not have a vote. Nor would he record one, or in the case of a motion carried, record the division. Lost motions, like details of the debates, simply were not mentioned. Thompson was exceedingly discreet, such being his orders; but he would have been anyway.

So they bowed to one another, and chatted a bit in groups in the yard for a while, and when they had entered the State House at the ringing of a hand-bell, like large, staid schoolboys, each took off his tricorn and tucked it under his left arm as he made for the seat assigned to him.

* * * * *

The chairs were comfortable, and it was a lovely room, large, the walls classically white but not severe. Two brass-fitted fireplaces faced its single door, but they would not be used today, for the moment that the door was shut—and it would be kept locked, the only doorman being on the outside—the room became an oven. There were tall, handsome windows, to be sure, but these, lest any part of the quarrel be heard by a passer in the yard, were shut—all save a little at the top of each. That narrow opening was enough to admit some slight stir of air, not much. It was also enough to admit a large number of horseflies from a livery stable across the street, a stable the stalls of which were the more pungent today because of the extreme, the suffocating, heat. The horseflies did well for themselves among delegates to the Second Continental Congress. Coats and breeches, camlet, sagathy, drugget, even in some cases satin, wouldn't let them pass; but they were dexterous in finding necks, and the silk of stockings was as nothing to them.

All through that which followed, for four days, the solemn discussion was to be punctuated by the slap of hands on horseflies.

On the wall at the back, facing the president's desk, was a panoply consisting of a drum, swords, and banners captured from Fort Ticonderoga the previous year when Ethan Allen and Benedict Arnold had pounced upon that place, the former shouting that they were taking it "in the name of the great Jehovah and the Continental Congress," from neither of which did they in fact hold any sort of commission. These martial trophies—trophies of a war that then had not yet become a war —and had it done so since?—might sometimes have been found inspiriting, but must more often have embarrassed the delegates. Fortunately their backs were turned to the panoply most of the time.

In the chair was John Hancock of Boston, one of the richest men in America, his fortune, inherited from an uncle—a loyalist, incidentally—being largely founded on smuggling. Hancock, the first man to have a house on Beacon Hill, was fussy, dressy, punctilious, pleased with himself. Fond of display, he was wont to parade the streets of Philadelphia in state, with all sorts of liveried servants behind him and before; and he was sometimes dubbed "King Hancock." Yet here was every inch a patriot! He might glory in the prominence of his position, but he carried himself carefully and well. He was one of the two men— Samuel Adams was the other—whom Gage had refused to include in a general offer of pardon. A great deal of his wealth was in the form of Boston houses, yet when Washington was considering a proposal to burn Boston John Hancock unhesitatingly urged him to do so. There were those who did not like the president's pretentiousness, his mannerisms, but no one had ever found any fault with the way he conducted the Second Continental Congress.

* * * * *

John Hancock. *Engraving made from a painting by Chappel.*

A convenient expression of the time was "out of doors." A thing that was done "out of doors" was done elsewhere, without ceremony or record, perhaps not literally in the open air but at least off the floor. "Out of doors" could be made to sound sinister or only rather playful, depending on the person who used it. It implied a deal of some sort, a prearrangement, conceivably though not necessarily evil.

The most prominent practitioner "out of doors" was Samuel Adams, a man who lived, breathed, and had his very being in chamber politics.

His was not an impressive figure. He was fifty-four, an advanced age in this group, near senility. His eyes watered. His hands shook, and his head habitually jerked back and forth. He was from Massachusetts, in itself a grievous fault. His clothes were inelegant. His manners, though technically impeccable—he was after all a Harvard graduate—were not such as to inspire confidence. Men were instinctively leery of him until they got to know him. He could write clearly, if not felicitously, and he had done a prodigious amount of patriotic journalism.[5] Though on occasion he could speak directly and even forcefully, he was no spellbinder. Neither was he a lawyer. The son of one of the founders of the Caulkers' Club,[6] his knowledge of practical, down-to-sidewalk politics was unsurpassed. But his reputation, having preceded him, hurt rather than helped him among the fashionable men in this city of fashion. His far-left views were too well known. He was thought a menace. "That Machiavel of Chaos," he had been called. Yet it may be significant that the first man with whom Samuel Adams tangled in Philadelphia, at the time of the convening of the first Continental Congress two years before, the great, the glittering Joseph Galloway, that brilliant lawyer, leader of the large Pennsylvania delegation, had, certainly at least in part because of the machinations of this same wobbly, shifty old man from Massachusetts, gone down to defeat. Sam Adams from the beginning had dared to advocate independence. Galloway had said: "Independency means ruin. If England refuses it, she will ruin us; if she grants it, we shall ruin ourselves."

Yet independence was coming; it was in the air; while Galloway, an outcast now, sat in London writing enlightened excuses. Galloway, who of course hated him, nevertheless gave Sam Adams credit for his persistence, describing him as a man "who eats little, drinks little, sleeps little, thinks much, and is most decisive and indefatigible in his objects."[7]

It was said of Samuel Adams that his only pomp was poverty, and he may even have been a bit childish about this, flaunting his rags. Such an attitude did no good at the Congress.

Samuel Adams.

Indeed, it probably was the chief thing that men held against him—that he was not a person of property.

Do not put it down to pride of purse! There were precious few snobs in the State House in Philadelphia this summer! But it must be remembered that "a stake in society" was the key to enfranchisement, and the only one. Property was prestige, and a man's political importance, potentially at least, was measured in terms of the land he owned. Every colony had a property qualification, and in seven of them it was limited to land, personal property and income being ignored. The theory was that the more a man had to lose, the more careful he would be in conducting the affairs of government, in which it was taken for granted that he would be offered a part. Sam Adams had nothing to lose—except, as his defenders might retort, his life. He was that most contemptible of American figures, the man who has failed in business. He had no head for figures, no financial ambition. He had inherited a fortune in cash, together with a prosperous maltery; but he soon spent the one—not recklessly, only absent-mindedly—and so mismanaged the other that he became bankrupt. He didn't care. He was more interested in the meetinghouse than the countinghouse. Friends got him a position as a Boston city tax collector, but he bungled this too. There was no hint of dishonesty, but there were shortages to be made up, and friends and relations did this for him. Thereafter nothing so prosaic as regular paid employment ever got between Sam Adams and his calling. Though he had a large family, he lived humbly, not to say frugally. His influence being what it was, and Crown political methods what *they* were, more than once he was offered large sums to keep his mouth shut; and he probably never even knew it. When he was elected to the First Continental Congress, it was incumbent upon his friends to chip in with a suit, stockings, a wig, a horse, money for his purse, perhaps even the purse itself. It is worthy of note that Sam Adams had such friends. He always did have.

Every effort had been made to get representatives of large fortunes into the Continental Congress. Men like Hancock, Washington, Charles Carroll, the Livingstons of New York, the

Lees and Nelsons of Virginia, were prizes. Even the lesser lights, by and large, were prosperous men. In such a company Sam Adams could hardly be expected to cut much of a figure. Yet he got things done—"out of doors."

* * * * *

The delegates to Congress were a snappish lot, split many ways for many reasons—religious, sectional, political. The southern and middle representatives, especially those from the proprietorial colonies, feared and hated the rambustious, opinionated New Englanders, "those Goths, those Vandals," who in their turn despised the idle, effete plantationers. And so it went. But the biggest cleavage of all, just at this time, the widest schism, was in the matter of independence.

Those who were for declaring independence immediately were known as the violent men, and those who counseled a cooling-off period were called the considerate men.

One of the stock arguments of the considerate men was that the colonies had many friends in England—friends in high places, who might yet save the situation, but who would be alienated by an open avowal of independence. This had a good ring and it appealed to many, though Jefferson thought it "pusillanimous."

Parliament in truth had heard many a passionate plea in behalf of the American colonies. There was Isaac Barré, an Irish colonel and a notably fierce one, in speech as in appearance: a massive man, he was dark of visage and habitually scowled, and one of his eyes had been shot out. Barré it was who had first used the phrase that the colonists came to apply to themselves, "sons of liberty." The average member of Parliament, whether Whig or Tory, had a really appalling store of ignorance about the colonies. It is doubtful that he even knew the color of the Americans' skin, much less the tilt of their minds. Barré was different. He had visited America, under Wolfe, under Braddock—that was where he had got his wound —and he could, and repeatedly and explosively did, assert that the colonists were human, an astounding statement. He fought for them with great ferocity, never resting. Once after a particularly savage attack on the ministry he turned aside for some refreshment, and a back-bencher was heard to murmur: "Does it eat biscuit? I thought it only ate raw flesh!"

Yet Barré, if fearless, was poor. Parliament was no place for a poor man if he also happened to be honest. Votes were, quite simply, no bones being made about it, bought; and the court party always could purchase a safe majority. In Ben Franklin's wry phrase, the royal M.P.'s had to be bribed "to vote according to their consciences." So it was too with Burke, who was wholeheartedly for the colonial cause, who indeed at one time was even a paid agent of New York, a somewhat startling sideline for a member. Burke was eloquent, and the benchers invariably listened to him, but there is no record that his splendiferous oratory ever changed an "aye" to a "nay."

Then there was John Wilkes, the "Wilkes and liberty" man, beloved in the colonies. But Wilkes was so erratic, even in that company of erratic, eccentric men; he was so dissolute, ugly—worst of all—brilliant, that he was distrusted by all but a few sycophants; and the King positively hated him. Wilkes—it was one of his few consistencies—never wavered in his support of the colonial cause; but it might be that his backing did more harm than good.

Pitt was a favorite of the colonists, who bought hundreds of statuettes and hideous mezzotints that showed him in classical costume benignly receiving the thanks of the American aborigines (who never heard of it) for his leadership in the repeal of the Stamp Act. Pitt, with his grandeur, his flashing gray eyes, his nose "that would cut a diamond," might refer to "those irritable and umbrageous people," but he was outspoken, and by no means brief, in his assertion that the colonists "are equally entitled with yourselves to all of the natural rights of mankind, and peculiar privileges of Englishmen; equally bound by its laws, and equally participating of the Constitution of this free country." Tellingly he could remind fellow parliamentaries that "the Americans are the sons, not the bastards of England." Oh, Mr. Pitt had been magnificent! But he was no longer Mr. Pitt. He was Lord Chatham now: the Great Commoner had become an earl. The effect of this, and of his acceptance of a royal pension of £3,000 a year, was terrific; for our statesman, despite his gifts, had little to fall back on in Parliament save his personal popularity. He still was listened to when, despite the poor health that caused him to be absent from London for months on end, he rose in his place, consenting to speak. He still gave off a gutty rumble like that of some great volcano. Steam rose from him. But there was no longer any lava.

Pitt had done more than any other one man to build up the British empire, and it is conceivable that, sick though he was, he might yet have succeeded somehow in saving the American colonies for the mother country if King George had made him first minister. But this was unthinkable. Pitt would never be called back. George III, a believer in "personal" government, wanted as ministers only servants who would obey his orders instantly and unquestioningly, whatever their own beliefs. Pitt was not that kind of man. So he spluttered in semi-retirement, picturesque but impotent.

These then were the principal friends in England of the American colonies—colorful men but quixotic, and not organized at all. On the whole, perhaps Thomas Jefferson was right.

True, the London merchants almost to a man were in favor of better treatment for the colonists, their best customers, and not afraid to say so. But the merchants had amazingly little weight just then. The court party was strong enough to ignore them; and anyway trade was looked down upon by exalted British statesmen as something nasty, degrading.

It was encouraging, also, to see the attitude of high British military men, even though they had little political influence. Lord Effingham had resigned his commission rather than take up arms against the colonists, and for the same reason Admiral Lord Keppel refused the American command. Thomas Gage had married an American woman and was openly in favor of the colonists, so he was withdrawn from Boston. General Amherst was hauled out of retirement, made a baron, and given his regiments back, after which he was offered the supreme command in America. He refused. He said flatly that the American colonies couldn't be conquered.

Something of the same sort happened in the case of General Henry Conway, a distinguished soldier, a member of the Commons, and younger brother of the Duke of Hertford. It was proposed to appoint him to supreme military command in America, but the King was warned in time, though unofficially, that Conway, if so appointed, would refuse to serve; and, moreover, such a refusal would mean even more among top military men than had that of Amherst.[8]

The brothers Howe then were put in charge. The sons of Viscount Howe of the Irish peerage and a female bastard of George I and the Baroness Kielmannsegge they were, therefore, first cousins once removed of George III himself. General William Howe, a large, dark, taciturn man with heavy features and bad teeth, was to command the land forces, while Admiral Lord Richard Howe, as tall and even darker—the sailors called him "Black Dick"—ruled those at sea. Their older brother, George, dead now—he was killed at Ticonderoga in '58—had been well liked by the colonists during his service in the French and Indian War, and perhaps this was why the surviving brothers were sent over. No other reason is apparent. These two were Whigs, sympathetic to the colonial cause; and though no doubt they meant to do a good job, they didn't affect enthusiasm.

* * * * *

The meeting was called to order, the door locked. Letters received the previous night were read aloud—from Generals Washington, Schuyler, Arnold, Sullivan, and some colonels as well. There were many of these, and all carried complaints. The clerk had a dry rasping voice, purposefully emotionless. The members slapped flies.

* * * * *

It had been almost a year ago that the Hichborne incident did so much to raise the general regard for independence—though it hardly seemed so at the time.

A second petition to the King (who had refused to receive the first) had been authorized and written, largely by John Dickinson, who sponsored it. The debate over this had been exceedingly bitter, though as usual a unanimous "aye" was recorded. Even John Adams voted for it, when it was clear that he had lost, though he snorted that it was "a measure of imbecility."

When the decision had been recorded, John Dickinson, "pale as ashes," though too much of a gentleman to gloat, nevertheless got to his feet. They had mauled his original message a bit: it was a way Congress had.

"Mr. President, there is only one word in this paper of which I disapprove, and that is the word 'Congress.'"

Immediately fat Ben Harrison rose.

"Mr. President, there is only one word in this paper of which I approve, and that is the word 'Congress.'"

It was passed all the same, an act that to the New Englanders and their Virginian friends was a show of weakness.

To Adams in his boardinghouse there came, a few nights later, a young man named Benjamin Hichborne. Hichborne lived in Boston and had been visiting relatives in Philadelphia. He would start back the next morning. Did Mr. Adams have any letters for him to carry? John Adams, who'd had a hard day, said "no," a word that came easily to his lips at any time. Hichborne persisted, and again Adams said "no." Then the truth came out. Hichborne worked in the law office of a man who was suspected of Tory sympathies, and in consequence the young clerk himself was so suspected, though in truth innocent. The slightest touch of that tar could ruin a man's reputation, his business as well. If it became known in Boston that Mr. Adams himself had entrusted this Hichborne with personal letters to some friend or some member of Mr. Adams' family, then he would automatically be cleared. Adams was touched, for he had a kind heart, something he was ordinarily careful to conceal. Tired, even more peevish than was his wont, annoyed by Dickinson, he sat down and wrote a short note to "dear Abbey," his wife, and a slightly longer one to General James

Warren, speaker of the Massachusetts House of Representatives. Warren was an old friend, and Adams let himself go:

> A certain great fortune and piddling genius, whose fame has been trumpeted so loudly, has given a silly cast to our whole doings. We are between hawk and buzzard. We ought to have had in our hands, a month ago, the whole legislative, executive, and judicial of the whole continent, and have completely modelled a constitution; to have raised a naval power, and opened all our ports wide; to have arrested every friend of government on the continent, and held them as hostages for the poor victims in Boston.... We are lost in the extensiveness of our field of business. We have a continental treasury to establish, a paymaster to choose, and a committee of correspondence, or safety, or accounts, or something, I know not what, that has confounded us all this day.

A few days later a ferry to Newport, Rhode Island, on which the returning law clerk was a passenger, was seized, for no reason that survives, by a British naval patrol. It seems that Hichborne made some attempt to destroy the letters he carried —though how he came to know that they were political dynamite is not clear—but in this he was too late; and, indeed, the attempt itself might have drawn attention to the letters, which in any event were taken from him. The letters were passed around in Newport. They were sent to Boston, where the delighted British released them to a Tory newspaper, the *Massachusetts Gazette*. Other newspapers picked them up, as was the custom. They had been subjected to "a little garbling," Adams was ruefully to admit, but he couldn't say how much because he had not kept copies. The originals were sent to London and published there; and the fact that in England the writer was generally supposed to be Samuel Adams, whose name was so much better known abroad[9], in no way lessened their effectiveness. The timing, though sheer chance, must have looked contrived. Here, on the one hand, was this newly received petition in which the colonists protested their undying adherence to the King, their devotion to the British constitution, while, on the other hand, there was a letter from one American statesman to another in which was set forth a demand for a separate constitution, for a navy, an independent treasury, a new bench, and all the rest of it. This only confirmed the English belief that the colonists had all along been plotting to set up a republic.

The effect at home was more immediate, and more personal. John Dickinson was a Quaker, and it may be assumed a good one, but even the friendly persuasion does not demand of its members that they be called "piddling genius" and like it. The next time John Adams met Dickinson in the street he lifted his hat politely, but Dickinson cut him dead; nor did they ever speak to one another again, save on the floor of Congress.

There were many others in Philadelphia who were dismayed and who tended to avoid John Adamss—or so he thought, for he was feeling very sorry for himself just at this time.

Yet the long-range effect might have been favorable to the cause of independence. At least the word had been spoken; and after the first shock many a man must have fallen to thinking what it would be like to have a navy, a treasury . . . John Adams' personal popularity had never stood so low, but the thing he loved most in this world was no longer unmentionable; and anyway he was used to being snubbed.

As for the petition, which was formally addressed to the king-in-parliament rather than the king on his throne, both Lords and Commons refused officially to receive it; and George III wouldn't even read the thing.

* * * * *

There were other letters—from the New Jersey convention assembled at that colony's capital, Burlington; from the New Hampshire convention; from the convention at Annapolis. This last was of great importance, though it caused no stir, for its contents had been known since yesterday.

The unit rule was in operation, as determined by the First Continental Congress two years ago. That is, each colony counted for one vote, and this vote was that of the majority of its delegates, regardless of numbers; if the delegates were split there was no vote counted for that colony. The delegates were appointed or elected in various ways, since there was no authority for the procedure anyway, and even those from Massachusetts probably did not represent a majority of the people. Those from Connecticut, New Jersey, New York, and Maryland had first been picked by committees of correspondence; those from Massachusetts, Rhode Island, Pennsylvania, and Delaware by legislative assemblies; each of the Carolinas had a convention; in New Hampshire the town deputies got together in caucus, originally.[10] These methods, however, were constantly being changed. The Continental Congress itself had no control over them.

Not the slightest pretense of listening to both sides ever was made when these delegates were named. In addition to the property qualification—and the simple fact that it cost a lot of money to go to faraway Philadelphia and serve your country for a few months or a few years—there was the paramount matter of local politics. Nobody will ever know the figures, but at the beginning of hostilities, although New England and Virginia had been Whig territory, New York and Georgia almost certainly had been Tory, and the other states at best were about even. Their delegations did not reflect this. No dyed-in-the-wool loyalist, to be sure, would have consented to serve on a patriots' committee or committee of safety (and it was these groups that had the most to say in the selection of Congressmen) even if he had been acceptable. The word democracy was never used. No doubt they all knew what it meant, but it was not thought of.

There was no limit to the size of a delegation. Currently, for instance, Pennsylvania had seven delegates, but it had nine a little while ago. New Hampshire had only two, and until lately only one, Josiah Bartlett, one of the most seriously overworked members, as he himself complained, because an unwritten house rule was to appoint one representative from each colony to each of the more important standing committees—which meant that Bartlett, poor man, was on all of them. Nor was the size of a given delegation likely to remain unchanged. There was no policy here. Congressmen could be reinforced or recalled by the colonial governments at any time without notice. They came and went. Many had urgent business or professional duties at home, or domestic duties. Others thought that just now, because of the great change-over, their provincial politics were more important than Congressional politics. Still others were with the army. Thus George Washington, an independencer now, was in New York preparing to encounter the foe. Thus Sullivan of New Hampshire, a tremendous fighter for freedom, was a brigadier in the field. Thus Christopher Gadsden, a rough, unsoutherly man who last February had gone back to South Carolina to help organize the militia; today in Philadelphia—for he was wholehearted in favor of independence—his presence would have been helpful, the South Carolina delegation being one of the doubtful ones. And Patrick Henry. He too was missing on this memorable occasion. Patrick Henry was a backwoodsman, determinedly uncouth, inexorably homespun, always afraid that one of his constituents might catch him looking into a book, or that he might sometime, inadvertently, quote Livy. He clung to an outlandish brogue: he would say "Cheena" for "China," the "yearth" for the "earth," and would refer to a man's "naiteral" parts being improved by "larnin' "; yet such was the force of his eloquence that men forgot this once he had started to speak. Patrick Henry was back in Virginia now, where he had become the first non-royal, the first *elected,* governor.

Originally most of the delegates were instructed by the body that named them to do this or that, or to refrain from doing it; and most of these sets of instructions contained a command to vote against separation, or independence, if by any horrid chance that proposal was made; while other delegates, though not so enjoined, felt that they should not take such a decisive step without a specific nod of assent from the governing body back home. It had been the patriots' part for some months now to get these instructions rescinded. Independence could not be proclaimed until they were.

New England was solid for independence. The South was showing firmer than had been expected. Pointing out that the great distance made it inadvisable to fetter delegates with instructions, Georgia—which had not even been represented in the First Continental Congress—first liberated hers, putting them on their own consciences. North Carolina actually had instructed hers to vote for independence. Virginia had long been in favor of it. Only South Carolina wavered.

The middle states were the patriots' chief worry.

New York was largely controlled by the clannish rich families, and though the Livingstons and the Schuylers were for independence, more or less, if not with any exuberance, the DeLanceys, DePeysters, and Van Cortlandts were dead-set against it. On June 8, when it had become certain as a result of the Congressional action of the previous day that a vote on separation was inevitable, the New York delegates had written for further instructions, pointing out: "the matter will admit of no delay." The provincial congress assembled in City Hall, New York, replied that it was "unanimously of opinion that you are not authorized by your instructions to give the sense of this colony on the question of declaring it to be, and continue, an independent State," adding that in truth most of the members of the said provincial congress didn't even think that they had the right so *to* instruct. New York was known as the most flagrantly Tory of all the colonies. However, a majority of the New York delegates—they numbered four at this time—now were personally in favor of independence. They had written again, urging that they be authorized to vote for it, pleading for a prompt reply. They had not yet received an answer and didn't think that they should take part in the debate, though they would certainly be present.

Pennsylvania was a separate problem, a serious one. It contained the largest city, presently the largest port, one of the biggest populations; and it was wealthy—and the host. Timothy Pickering, a testy party at best, called it "the enemy's country." Not for nothing had it been named the Keystone Colony, though New York might have been given the same name: between them they formed the center of the arch made by the seaboard colonies; and if the South was separated from New

England—this of course was the grand strategy behind the Howe expedition—there could be no hope of separate survival. Pennsylvania was approximately one-third Quakers, one-third German Lutherans. The remainder were mostly Scotch-Irish Presbyterians. The Germans (the "Pennsylvania Dutch") were largely farmers of fairly recent arrival, men who had never before enjoyed anywhere near so much political and religious liberty as they had found here, and who in consequence could hardly be expected to wax excited about independence, though they might generally favor it. Moreover, they were not organized. The large, wealthy Quaker families had always controlled the colony, a proprietorial one. The Quakers—"puling pusillanimous cowards" Sam Adams thought them—were not so mild as might have been expected. Only a few of the most orthodox would be likely to refuse to bear arms in any circumstances. Most of the so-called Free Quakers would fight if it could be proved to them that fighting was necessary in self-defense; but they were cautious men, stubborn men moreover, who had a great deal to lose. The Scotch-Irish on the whole were an aggrieved folk, thinking themselves withheld from a fair share of government. Indeed, a local revolution was in progress in Pennsylvania, upstairs in this very building. On June 10, after some pointed, not to say belligerent, demonstrations on the part of the militia, the Assembly had met—without a quorum, two-thirds. Neither was there a quorum the next day, or the next. The legislators probably were afraid, and not without reason. June 13 there was at last a quorum, but nothing was done .The threats got thicker. June 14, at 3 P.M., the Assembly formally if unenthusiastically removed the anti-independence restrictions of the previous November, setting the Pennsylvania delegates free to vote as they pleased.[11] Still the patriots were not satisfied, and on June 18 there was a meeting in Carpenter's Hall of the committees of safety from all over the state, a meeting that resolved "that the present Government of this Province is not competent to the exigencies of our affairs," and called for a new convention "on the authority of the People alone," whatever that meant. The election of delegates by this convention, though already imminent, on Monday, July 1, 1776, had not yet been held. Meanwhile, the seven delegates from Pennsylvania, though released, remained opposed to immediate independence, only one, Benjamin Franklin, being in its favor, though Morton, a farmer of Swedish extraction, was believed to be wobbling, and James Wilson, that small, smart, bespectacled Scottish real estate man, was less sure of himself than before.

Delaware had three delegates, two of whom were for independence, but one of these—a brigadier, Caesar Rodney—was absent in Dover on militia business. If it came to a division today McKean would surely vote for it, Read as surely would vote against—and Delaware would not be recorded one way or the other.

In New Jersey too there had been a political upset, and the radicals, the impatient men, had taken over—the sort of thing that had happened or was happening, to a greater or less degree, in each of the colonies. Only a couple of weeks ago Congress had been notified of the arrest of the royal governor of New Jersey, and the new men in power at Burlington had withdrawn the three delegates, appointing five new ones— Richard Stockton, the handsome chief justice of the state; Dr. John Witherspoon, president of the College of New Jersey (at a place called Princeton), a lank learned divine from Scotland; tiny excitable Francis Hopkinson, poet, painter (he had been a pupil of Benjamin West), attorney, harpsichordist; John Hart, a sixty-five-year-old farmer, originally from Stonington, Connecticut; and Abraham Clark, a waspish small lawyer from Elizabethtown. These men had been told to vote for independence "if you shall find it necessary or expedient." They had hurried off, for they sensed the need for haste, and two days ago, drenched with rain, they had arrived at the State House in Philadelphia and presented their credentials. They were eager, agog, a curious quintet, at first meek. They asked to hear the arguments for independence, and when it was pointed out to them that those arguments had been printed in every newspaper and spoken on every street corner in the land, they replied that they still wished to hear them from, as they might have said, the horse's mouth. Edward Rutledge, appealed to, in turn appealed to John Adams as the natural spokesman of the independence movement.

This Rutledge was the youngest person present, being twenty-six, but in point of service he was the senior member of the South Carolina delegation, the youngest in average of the Congress. Until a little while ago when his brother John quit Philadelphia to return to Charleston and the organization of a new state government, Edward, the younger of the two, had been somewhat overshadowed. This was so no longer. There was nothing shy about Edward Rutledge, and nothing apathetic. He talked through his nose, and talked often and positively, permitting no one to forget that he had studied law in London. Why Rutledge should be speaking up for the New Jersey delegation is not clear; but it was like him, who always mixed into others' affairs.

Adams didn't like Rutledge, who, he had confided to his diary, was "a perfect Bob-o-Lincoln—a swallow, a sparrow, a peacock, excessively vain, excessively weak . . . jejune, inane, and puerile." Half playfully he had protested that he was tired of going over those same arguments again, and that he would feel like a gladiator or a paid actor performing before an audience. Still, Rutledge persuaded him to do it. The men from New Jersey had listened carefully, and it was clear that they had approved; they would vote the right way.

After the first momentous debate on independence June 10, the Maryland delegates, personally for independence but hampered by "anti" instructions, wrote to the committee of safety at Annapolis asking that a convention be called "to give the explicit Sense of the Province on this Point . . . in this most important and interesting affair." It was the familiar story: the Congressmen, afire in Philadelphia, catching the spirit of the times, were well ahead of the men who had sent them. From Annapolis on the twenty-first came a plea for more time, but this was sternly denied by Congress. Here was a moment when procrastination might be fatal. If the ship of liberty was indeed to be launched it must be launched at the very top of the tide.

It was at this point in the game that Samuel Chase decided to quit Philadelphia and get back into the home field, where his services were needed. He was a burly, violent man, and they called him Bacon-Face because of his complexion. A lawyer from Annapolis, loud and rude, he was not popular with the rest of the Maryland delegates, who were quiet, rich, sophisticated men of the fox-hunting class; but he was a prodigious fighter for independence. Two nights ago, exhausted but exultant, he had sat down to write to John Adams that at long last the thing had been done—the Maryland convention, meeting in Annapolis, had voted to instruct the Maryland delegates for independence. The new instructions were even then being drawn up; and, indeed, the next day the impetuous Sam Chase himself rode the whole distance to Philadelphia with those instructions.

It was the formal, official announcement of this decision, from the convention itself, the paper Chase had brought, that Charles Thompson read this morning; and if it caused some smiles it brought no gasps, for Adams had long ago spread the tidings.

It was getting hotter in the room all the time.

The Congress voted to allot an aide-de-camp to a certain brigadier general.

Another letter from General Washington was read, and this and all of the other military epistles were duly referred to the Board of War.

Not until then did the independence resolutions come up.

* * * * *

When Parliament and King alike spurned the colonies' second petition, the breach had become steadily—and swiftly—wider. Indeed, the situation threatened to degenerate into a snarling match. The British were cooped up in Boston, unable to move by land, and cannons were being floated and sledded there from Ticonderoga. The speeches were more truculent than ever, the gestures wilder, but troops were being raised all through the colonies, and drilled, and trained; and gunpowder and lead, muskets too, were being smuggled in from a France that blandly assured England it knew nothing of such a trade. On December 6, 1775, Congress had openly disavowed allegiance to the British Parliament, though still at that time professing loyalty to the King. On the twenty-second of that month Parliament removed the colonies from the protection of the Crown, forbade all trade with them, and authorized the seizure of American ships: this was the nearest that either side ever got to a formal declaration of war. One of the cool, considerate men, James Wilson of Pennsylvania, could raise a majority for his resolution of January 9, 1776, denying any intent of independency; but it is doubtful that anyone on the other side of the sea took this seriously, convinced as they were over there that they were dickering with hypocrites; and the effect among the independencers, after their first outburst of disgust, was to cause them to strengthen their ranks. For example, Thomas Cushing of Massachusetts, who had voted for the Wilson measure, was called back and replaced by a staunch independence man, Elbridge Gerry.[12]

March 17, after Washington had fortified Dorchester Heights, the British cleared out of Boston. They had never meant to hold the city, an expensive one for them—New York, the place for which they were bound, would be of much greater strategic value—but it was a moral victory for the continentals, a much needed one, too, in view of the tragic news from Canada.

The Canadian failure—it could hardly be called a fiasco—was the more bitter just at this time because the business had started so briskly. It had been almost unbelievably bold, to begin with; and no doubt it would never have been authorized had not the prevailing belief in the colonies been that the French Canadians almost to a man would welcome a chance to fight England again, to throw off their "shackles."

It had been a two-pronged invasion, and most energetically

met, nor had the residents been as co-operative as had been hoped. Montreal, true, had been taken; but Quebec looked stronger than ever after the American general Montgomery was killed there, leaving Benedict Arnold in command. These two were brilliant men, as was Carleton, the Britisher, but even more effective in the long run was the redoubtable General Winter. The colonials were campaigning a long way from their base. Congress had been swamped with appeals for reinforcements, for more supplies. It had responded as best it could, but the news was uniformly bad, for the Indians had fallen in with the British, the navy was active, and Burgoyne had recently taken command with enormous reinforcements, including Hessians. An investigating committee had been sent to Canada, and its report too had been a cold douche for the Congress. Washington could not possibly spare another man to the north; he had already done far more than most generals would have, digging in at New York as he was, against that certain invasion from the sea. It seemed as though nothing less than a miracle could keep Burgoyne from taking Lake Champlain and Lake George and pouring on down the Hudson with an irresistible host, to meet with Howe at New York, cutting the colonies in half.

April 6 Congress had opened the colonial ports, a measure that in itself was almost a declaration of independence, since it invited other nations to deal with us as a separate state, selling us the things without which we would perish:

> That any goods, wares, and merchandise, except such as are of the growth, production or manufacture of, or brought from any country under the dominion of the King of Great Britain, and except East India Tea, may be imported from any other parts of the world to the thirteen United Colonies, by the inhabitants thereof, and by the people of all such countries as are not subjects of the said King...

A significant change was to be noted in the colonial attitude toward George III. Until now it had been the custom to pretend to put all the blame for injustices done to the colonies upon Parliament or the cabinet, preferably the cabinet, and to maintain the fiction that the King himself was blameless, a well-meaning man misled by advisors. Perhaps distance—nothing else could have done it—lent enchantment to the head of the House of Hanover.

George was a waddling, unhandy man with pop-out eyes and a big behind. He had a habit of snapping quick, stupid questions, to which he gave no time for reply. "What?" he'd shout, leaning forward. "What?" He had the intelligence and capacities of a back-country fox-hunter. His had been an unfortunate childhood—a fool for a father, a lout for a grandfather, and a mother who was overprotective to the point of mania. As a person, then, it is possible to feel sorry for George III. As a king he was wholly despicable. He did not even have the excuse of inexperience: he had been sixteen years on the throne, a place for which he had been trained since babyhood. If he had been willing to be a royal figurehead like his grandfather, George II, and his great-grandfather, George I, if he had been content to reign without trying to rule, this indictment would not need to be so harsh. But the instinct of the colonists was right. George III was the proper villain of the piece. He insisted upon doing everything himself, in his own way. "Be king, Georgie, be king," his mother had drilled into him; and he was a dutiful son.

The Americans were beginning to understand this, and the colonial tone became more severe. The royal proclamation of December 22, 1775, which in effect outlawed the colonies, had done as much as any one thing to bring about this change of attitude. Even at a distance of three thousand miles it is not pleasant to be cut.

The change was a telling one, for now the cause had been dramatized. It was so much easier, and more satisfying, to jeer at a single, elaborately accoutered, physically unattractive man, than at a series of powdered, perfumed ministers whose names and titles were so curiously intermixed, and who in any event wouldn't be there long, for they shifted like the colors thrown

July 4, 1776

King George III.

by a kaleidoscope. The Prohibitory Act of December 22, which caused such umbrage in the colonies, in truth was an Act of Parliament, though issued in the King's name, but it was publicly supposed to have been the King's own doing, and at least it was not contrary to his wishes.

This might have been cause enough, but it was quickly followed by another—a stunning, unexpected stroke. The very day (January 9) that Wilson was pushing his no-independence resolution through Congress, there was published in that same city of Philadelphia an extraordinary book.

Thomas Paine was an Englishman who had come to these shores a few scant months ago and, until *Common Sense,* had lived journalistically, precariously, unknown. A bankrupt corset manufacturer, a cashiered customs collector, he had also made a failure of marriage. Nobody, probably not even himself, suspected that he had genius.

To liken *Common Sense* to a bombshell or a prairie fire would be flat. It was more than either. About 22,000 words long, red-faced, vulgar, magnificent, it was published both as a paperback and as a hard-cover book here and abroad in edition after edition. The authorized official sale in the colonies alone in the first year of publication—there were pirated editions besides—came to about 150,000.[13] It is safe to say that every person in America who could read had read it, while most of the others had caused it to be read to them.

Common Sense could not have been more appropriately titled. It minced no words but went right to the heart of the matter, sweeping aside, with the angry impatience of a man who has walked into a cobweb in the dark, the moralizing, the equivocations, the Latin tags and classical parallels, the hairsplitting so dear to the hearts of pamphleteers. It wasn't eloquent, it wasn't balanced. It was in execrable taste. But it stung.

Why monarchy? demanded Paine. What have we to do with that "most prosperous invention the devil ever set on foot for the promotion of idolatry?"

It had been the convention until this time, no matter how

slanderous the pamphlet, at least to keep the outer forms of politeness, especially when dealing with the royal house. Paine would have none of this.

There is something exceedingly ridiculous in the composition of monarchy; it first excludes a man from the means of information, yet empowers him to act in cases where the highest judgment is required. The state of a king shuts him from the world, yet the business of a king requires him to know it thoroughly.

Divine right?

A French bastard, landing with an armed banditti, and establishing himself King of England against the consent of the natives, is in plain terms a very paltry, rascally original. It certainly hath no divinity in it.

Common Sense came at exactly the right time; and if this was due to chance rather than design, it was none the less effective.

But Britain is the parent country, say some. Then the more shame upon her conduct. Even brutes do not devour their young, nor savages make war upon their families . . .

In England a king hath little more to do than make war and give away places; which, in plain terms, is to impoverish the nation and set it together by the ears. A pretty business, indeed, for a man to be allowed eight hundred thousand sterling a year for, and worshipped into the bargain.

The note of urgency was sounded throughout. The words fairly screamed for speed, speed.

. . . the period of debate is closed. Arms, as a last resource, must decide the contest . . .

By referring the matter from argument to arms, a new era for politics is struck; a new method of thinking hath risen. All plans, proposals, etc., prior to the nineteenth of April, i.e., to the commencement of hostilities, are like the almanacs of last year; which, though proper then, are superseded and useless now . . .

> Wherefore, since nothing but blows will do, for God's sake, let us come to a final separation, and not leave the next generation to be cutting throats, under the violated, unmeaning names of parent and child . . .
>
> There is ten times more to dread from a patched-up connection than from independence.

He had a point there. More and more of the colonists were coming to the realization that they had gone too far to turn back—or even to stop. Any kind of compromise at this juncture, even if it were possible, might, in Paine's phrase, "leave the sword to our children."

An appeal to natural law would have a powerful pull, as he knew:

> . . . there is something very absurd in supposing a continent to be perpetually governed by an island. In no instance hath nature made the satellite larger than its primary planet; and as England and America, with respect to each other, reverse the common order of nature, it is evident that they belong to different systems: England to Europe—America to itself.

This very strong argument—strong because so perfectly attuned to the times, which stood in awe of the "natural law"—had in addition a popular geographical appeal. The American colonists were inordinately fond of that word "continental." It had something grand about it, especially when juxtaposed to the "insular" of Great Britain.

It was sometimes said of George III—as sometimes it was too of Philip II of Spain—that he wasn't vicious, wasn't bad at bottom; that it was his misfortune, merely, to be a man of mean talents and narrow outlook, whose pettiness shone the more, like a rotten mackerel in the moonlight, because of the glare of his position. Thomas Paine took no such namby-pamby stand. To him George III was "a hardened, sullen-tempered Pharaoh . . . the royal brute of Britain."

"Of more worth is one honest man to society, and in the sight of God," he wrote, "than all the crowned ruffians that ever lived."

Strong words. Yet the colonists were learning, it could be to their own amazement, that they were ready for them.

* * * * *

The two sides no longer were drifting toward war—a war that each believed would be a short one—but fairly *rushing* there. Two tremendous pushes were given, almost simultaneously, in the middle of the month of May.

On the tenth there was proposed from the floor of Congress a resolution urging the separate colonies to set up their own governments. In itself this was not new, though the resolution went further than Congress had gone before. What touched off one of the most furious debates in the history of that highly combustible body was the preamble:

Whereas his Britannic Majesty, in conjunction with the lords and commons of Great Britain, has, by a late act of Parliament, excluded the inhabitants of these United Colonies from the protection of his crown; And whereas, no answer, whatever, to the humble petitions of the colonies for redress of grievances and reconciliation with Great Britain, has been or is likely to be given; but, the whole force of that kingdom, aided by foreign mercenaries, is to be exerted for the destruction of the good people of these colonies; And whereas, it appears absolutely irreconcilable to reason and good Conscience, for the people of these colonies now to take the oaths and affirmations necessary for the support of any government under the crown of Great Britain, and it is necessary that the exercise of every kind of authority under the said crown should be totally suppressed, and all the powers of colonies, for the preservation of internal peace, virtue, and good order, as well as for the defence of their lives, liberties, and properties, against the hostile invasions and cruel depredations of their enemies; therefore, resolved . . .

They fought for five days, but at last it was passed—"unanimously."

James Duane was made angry by this, which was not characteristic of the man, one of the cool considerate ones, a New

York lawyer, plump, jolly, a dresser but a hard worker, a person presently engaged in the thankless task of trying to make real money grow where only paper had grown before. It was sure that he was no Tory; but he was young, with his fortune to make—he'd accumulated a great deal of property, had good connections, and had married into the Livingstons. He didn't wish to see the Congress do anything precipitant. His attitude was: "Let this ever be considered as a *family quarrel, disgraceful* and *ruinous*, into which we are innocently plunged by intolerable oppression, and which we are sincerely disposed to appease and reconcile . . . consistent with the preservation of our just rights."[14] In the corridor after the voting Mr. Duane encountered John Adams, who had written that preamble at the last minute, and whom he regarded intently now (Duane was slightly cross-eyed but there was nothing *sinister* in his aspect).

"Sir, I think that this is an instrument for manufacturing independence!"

Adams permitted himself a smile, one of the few times this had happened. Here was a high moment in his life.

"Sir, I think it is independence itself," he replied. "But," he added, "we must have it with more formality yet."

On that same day, May 15, Virginia commanded its delegates to *propose* "to declare the United Colonies free and independent States." North Carolina the previous month had instructed its delegates "to *concur* with the Delegates of the other colonies in declaring Independency"; but this was something else again, this *propose*.

It would come up on the floor. Congress would have to face it. No matter how hot the debate, nor how long, no matter how sedulously it was kept secret, sooner or later Congress would have to make up its collective mind and announce the result to a waiting world.

No time was lost. Richard Henry Lee was the head of the Virginia delegation in Philadelphia, an older man than his confrere Jefferson, and handsomer; a better talker too, more skilled in the intricacies of parliamentary politics; but it was because of seniority that Lee held his position, and to him was automatically entrusted the duty of proposing independence everywhere in America.

He rose on June 7, and presented three resolutions:

That these United Colonies are, and of a right ought to be, free and independent States, that they are absolved from all allegiance to the British Crown, and that all political connection between them and the State of Great Britain is, and ought to be, totally dissolved.

That it is expedient forthwith to take the most effectual measures for forming foreign Alliances.

That a plan of confederation be prepared and transmitted to the respective Colonies for their consideration and approbation.

It was the custom, though no rule, not to decide upon a significant problem the day it was presented. This resolution, then, without comment was held over until the following day, a Saturday.

It was debated, and fiercely, all day Saturday and all day Monday, June 10. No poll was made, for the discussion took place not in the Continental Congress as such but in the committee of the whole house, of which Benjamin Harrison was chairman, John Hancock stepping down, though all the other members stayed in the same seats, while Thompson, the secretary, of course made no record of these proceedings.

On the motion of Edward Rutledge, late that Monday afternoon, the committee of the whole reported to itself in the form of the Continental Congress, Hancock being back in the chair, a recommendation that the matter be postponed for three weeks, to be taken up again Monday, July 1. To this Congress gravely agreed.

Here was no victory for the cool, considerate men! If they could have forced the thing to a settlement they would have done so—to see it defeated by the very fact of division. The vote, strictly unofficial, stood: *For*, New Hampshire, Massachusetts, Rhode Island, Connecticut, Virginia, North Carolina, and Georgia; *Against*, Pennsylvania, New Jersey, Maryland,

South Carolina; *No Vote,* New York and Delaware, the former because of lack of instructions, the latter because of a split.

It was agreed by the cool and the violent alike, and the in-betweens, if there were any in-betweens, that this was no way to go before the world. Union or nothing was the watchword.

Throughout those three weeks, then, until this morning, Monday, July 1, 1776, the Lee Resolutions (the first was the key, of course, the other two following naturally) lay on the secretary's desk like a lighted bomb with a long fuse. Nobody mentioned them, at least on the floor, but they were never far from everyone's mind.

Meanwhile Maryland and New Jersey had been won over to the immediate cause. Some slight dent had been made in the strongest "anti" group, that of Pennsylvania. New Yorkers had not yet received any alteration of orders, and must abstain. Delaware remained split, but the third delegate from that colony, currently in Dover on militia duty, was Caesar Rodney, a convinced separationist; and Thomas McKean, a man with a thin face, a hawk's nose, and the hot eyes of a fanatic, had whispered the word that he would dispatch a messenger to fetch Caesar. He'd come all right, McKean promised. He'd come. Finally, it was believed that South Carolina might be vacillating.

This was the situation when John Hancock stepped down and Benjamin Harrison took the chair for a meeting of the committee of the whole.

* * * * *

The Goths of old Germany, Tacitus tells us, used to discuss twice in council any matter of moment to their state—once when drunk, once when sober. With no wish to be irreverent, a touch of this spirit in the Second Continental Congress might not have done much harm. For these gentlemen were deliberate, their proceedings marked by a deadly seriousness. Admirable they surely were, but it cannot be denied that sometimes they were very solemn.

There were a few exceptions, the most notable being Benjamin Franklin, a man who loved his fun, who simply couldn't open his mouth, even on a portentous occasion of state, without uttering some outrageous pun or jest. "We must all hang together," legend has John Hancock crying one day when the delegates seemed to be getting out of hand. "Assuredly we must," Dr. Franklin was heard to say, "for if we don't we'll all hang separately." The story has never been authenticated; but it *might* be true; it's like Franklin.

Another exception to the prevailing solemnity was the man Harrison, sometimes called Falstaff. Each of the chairmen was in his thirties, but Harrison was as fat as Hancock was thin, sloppy where Hancock was prim, a great winesack of a man who would roar at his own jokes, most of which were bawdy. Wealthy, a Virginia planter, he was a person of good education, good "background"; but he liked to cover this. When he was in the chair the sessions were lively. He loved good brandy as he loved good food, and plenty of both, but most of all he loved to lampoon his fellow delegates. Once he told the tiny, peppery Elbridge Gerry, who had a tendency to stammer when excited, that he, Harrison, had less to fear from the end they'd probably all come to, since he was so heavy that he would lose consciousness at the very drop itself, whereas the little man from Massachusetts might dangle for half an hour before he died. Gerry was not amused.

* * * * *

Our villain here, a most improbable one, is John Dickinson. A man of high moral convictions, he could not have sneered if his life depended upon it. Moderation was his forte, and his rectitude never had been called to question; though of late it was being whispered that he had changed position, becoming almost—it was a word you used of anybody you disliked—a Tory. This was unfair. The American colonists were changing, the American people, but not John Dickinson.

Forty-three, he was tall, slender, pale, richly dressed for a Friend—for he was in fact a rich man, a successful lawyer, a third-generation landowner who was passionately attached to his seat Fairhill, on the outskirts of the city. It was sometimes said of him that he was henpecked, and this too was unfair.

He was a devoted family man, and it was no secret that his wife and daughters urged him to stay out of politics, fearing for his health and fortune, even for his life; but all the women in all the world could not have swayed John Dickinson from what he took to be his duty. A brilliant parliamentarian, he was equally skilled "out of doors." He suffered from a hot temper, hard to hold in control, and suffered too from what Sydney Smith was to call the only enemy he did not like to have at his feet—gout. Dickinson could not be ignored; neither could he be browbeaten. Since the hurried departure for England of his opponent Joseph Galloway, Dickinson had been the undisputed leader of the Pennsylvania delegation, the largest as it was the most influential in Congress.

To Philadelphians John Dickinson's wealth, his professional standing, his family—his mother was a Cadwalader—were of paramount importance. The rest of the world knew him as an author. He was called the penman of the Continental Congress. He had written the declaration of rights issued by the Stamp Act Congress, and the first petition to the King in 1775, papers which, if they had no effect on the ministry or the King, at least were much admired in Parliament, where it had not hitherto been supposed that anybody in the American colonies could express himself so well. When it came time to frame a declaration on taking arms, in July of the previous year, the Congress appointed as an assistant for Dickinson Mr. Jefferson of Virginia, who had taken his seat only two days before. Jefferson's reputation as a writer was local, limited, not international like Dickinson's. Nevertheless he was allowed to write the declaration on taking up arms, and indeed he wrote it twice—and Congress turned down both versions. After that it seemed no more than natural that John Dickinson should take over the task and produce another masterpiece. It was a pity that young Mr. Jefferson's feeling had to be hurt; but he kept his peace.

Dickinson's best-known work, however, was not a state paper but a pamphlet, *Letters from a Farmer in Pennsylvania to the Inhabitants of the British Colonies,* published nine years ago and still being talked about. Cogent, pithy, eminently sensible in its exposition of the colonists' woes, it was as much admired abroad as at home. The great Mr. Pitt condescended to praise it. So did Voltaire. Philadelphia was proud, and properly, of the *Letters,* and John Dickinson was pointed out to visitors in the street.[15]

"Let us behave like dutiful children, who have received unmerited blows from a beloved parent," Dickinson had written. "Let us complain to our parent; but let our complaints speak at the same time the language of affection and veneration."

That was his attitude then, in 1767, as it was still his attitude today. It mattered not that the tide had turned, that now he stood almost alone. He was Canute. He would rebuke the tide, causing it to ebb.

Dickinson was one of those liberal Quakers known as Free Quakers; but he *was* a Quaker.

Of all the divisions, sectional squabbles, jealousies, and suspicions that tended to keep the thirteen colonies apart, causing many well-wishers on both sides of the sea sadly to predict that if ever the colonists did win their independence they would tear one another to pieces and end in chaos, only to be taken back by Britain on humiliating terms, or else snatched up by some other European power—of all these, religion was the most explosive.

"Government is dissolved," Patrick Henry had cried at the time of the First Continental Congress. "We are in a state of nature, sir! The distinctions between Virginians, Pennsylvanians, New Yorkers, and New Englanders are no more."

This was roundly applauded then and much quoted afterward; but it was words; and the condition continued.

In 1775 there had been in the colonies these churches: Congregational 668, Presbyterian 588, Angelican 495, Baptist 494, Quaker 310, German Reformed 159, Lutheran 150, Dutch Reformed 120, Methodist 65, Catholic 56, Moravian 31, Congregational-Separatist 27, Dunker 24, Mennonite 16, French Protestant 7, Sandemanian 6, Jewish 5, Rogerene 3.[16] These figures are not completely significant, since they give no idea of the varying sizes of the congregations and, even more telling, their distribution.

The Congregationalists were largely confined to New England, the Quakers to Pennsylvania, while the Anglican church, though represented in every colony, had its greatest strength in the South. What toleration might be found was, by and large, in the Middle Colonies; and it was little enough. Pennsylvania was the least bigoted, being, in the matter of Roman Catholicism for example, even more liberal than Maryland.[17]

The differences, as far as the Continental Congress was concerned, were regional, social, rather than religious; but they *seemed* religious.

The Anglicans disliked and distrusted the puritanical New Englanders for their "leveling" methods, their scorn of the differences in rank, and their assumption that they knew everything: "the wise men of the East," Braxton of Virginia called them, while others referred to them as "the saints." That attitude of "he who is not with me is agin me" did not appeal to the men of the plantations, many of whom had studied English constitutional law at the Middle Temple in London. They were willing enough to take a bold course, but stridency they deplored. Couldn't a man be a patriot without being vulgar? Before meeting the New Englanders at Philadelphia, what they had chiefly heard of them had to do with street mobs, impassioned speeches, barn-burnings, lynchings. This sort of thing did not go down well with gentlemen whose homes were largely occupied and surrounded by slaves.

For their part, the New Englanders none too discreetly despised the pomp of the Anglican church, its ritual, candles, incense, stained glass, which smacked of Rome. They took these things much more heavily than did the men who were "subjected" to them. The truth is, the Anglican church in America, despite statistics, was not strong, and membership in it might be a matter of habit rather than one of conviction. It was, bluntly, something less than a stepchild of the mother church in England, and its members were no more than human when they resented this. For no reason that anyone knew, all thirteen colonies were in the see of London and had been from the beginning; yet no bishop of London, nor any other bishop, ever had visited any of them. Time after time the suggestion that a bishopric be created in the colonies was rejected, brusquely too.[18] The bishops in the House of Lords, without fail and as one man, had voted in support of the head of their church, King George, opposing every colonial petition, every effort to get justice; and this did little to raise the standing of their establishment in America. Colonial candidates for ordination were obliged, at their own expense, to travel six thousand miles. One petition pointed out that, in the year 1767, of the fifty-two would-be priests who did this, ten died on the voyage or from its results. Understandably the high churchmen of England were reluctant to deny holy orders to men who had made such a sacrifice—men about whom they could learn little—and for this reason some weak ones got through, again lowering the church's prestige in the colonies. This condition made for a shortage of clergy here, and those there were were vehemently "English." The men from Massachusetts cried out that many of the most prominent loyalists— Samuel Seabury, Miles Cooper, Samuel Auchmuty, Samuel Peters, Charles Inglis, Thomas Bradbury Chandler, Jonathan Boucher—were Anglican divines.[19] What the Massachusetts men did not understand was that these and others like them were by no means as representative of their flocks as were the Congregational pastors of New England. About half of the men present in the State House the first of July, 1776, were Anglicans; but no matter what their priests might say or do or write, or their far-off bishop, they would vote each according to his own conscience.

The Anglicans and Congregationalists were the giants. Smaller groups, for the most part, asked only to be left alone. Excepting the Quakers, they could not have done much if they'd wished to. The colonial laws forbade. There was no Jew in the State House the day the question of independence came up. Neither was there a Roman Catholic.[20]

Of all the jealousies and suspicions that separated the colonies from one another, the distrust of the Virginians for the "levelling" Massachusetts man—atheists in their eyes, all but anarchists—was the most disruptive. Gestures of conciliation had been and were being made; but resentment still was there, deep.

Virginians and Bostonians alike, however, could turn on the Quaker with the charge that he persisted, ostrich-like, in denying the existence of a great and present peril, that his meekness and patience were carried to dangerous lengths. The *logic* of the Quakers was irritating enough; their prodigious *stubbornness* was even more so.

When the committee of the whole house was called to order, then, and John Dickinson got the floor, there must have been many a bitter, tight, if silent, sigh. Doggedly the delegates leaned back to listen.

* * * * *

There was nothing said in that beautiful room July 1 that had not been said there a hundred times before. These men were unlikely to be moved by oratory. They knew one another too well. Yet they were aware that the eyes of mankind were upon them, and so they went once more through the whole wearisome, world-shaking debate.

This was not a continuation but rather a repetition of the historic discussion of June 10, when a vote on the Lee resolutions at last had been postponed for three weeks. That is, the arguments were the same. There were, however, differences in personalities, or the weight of personalities, and there was a decided difference in the *tone*.

Duane of New York, a strong moderation man, was not present. Young Robert Livingston, another, had lately been recalled by New Jersey, the new delegation of which clearly and even eagerly favored an immediate declaration. Maryland no longer was a block. Its energetic Sam Chase had returned to Annapolis, but the others, William Paca and Thomas Stone, had new instructions: they would vote for the measure. Old Joseph Hewes of North Carolina had gone over to the independence camp suddenly, dramatically, making that colony sure. The New York delegates remained under orders not to vote for any form of independence, but their state convention was to assemble in a few days, at which time it seemed certain that those orders, already a year old, would be revoked; and meanwhile the New York delegates at least would not vote *against* the Lee resolutions. South Carolina still was opposed, but the leader, Edward Rutledge, for once did not seem certain of himself.

As it had been from the beginning, Pennsylvania was the crucial colony. Ben Franklin had but a single vote, but he was a powerful worker "out of doors," and he or somebody else had won over old Judge Morton. Allen and Biddle, arch conservatives, fearing to be pushed to the verge, had resigned. Robert Morris, the merchant, and his partner, Thomas Willing, were opposed, but they were not men to raise their voices on the floor. Humphries was unalterably opposed; and then there was Dickinson himself. James Wilson took the floor to plead in vain for another postponement, but it was generally believed that in the event of a showdown he would plump for independence, reasoning, as he did, that the forthcoming convention undoubtedly would elect delegates pledged to independence—in other words, that independence had become the will of the people of Pennsylvania.

Dr. Witherspoon of Princeton spoke, declaring that the country was "not only ripe for the measure but in danger of rotting for the want of it."Wilson spoke again, pleading again, somewhat pathetically, for delay. John Adams spoke, of course, having called upon the shades of Demosthenes and Cicero to stand with him. And there were others. But it was John Dickinson who held forth at greatest length that hot, close day, and it was to him that the congressmen gave their most alert attention. He had prepared his speech well, for he was a careful man.

None of the moderates, not even Dickinson himself, any longer argued *against* independence. It was, now, simply a matter of *when*. On the tenth it had been asserted more than once that a comparatively small percentage of the people had any wish for independence, which was too momentous a matter to be settled out-of-hand by such a small group of delegates so imperfectly instructed; but since that time instructions had been changed, delegations too, in such a way that this argument had lost whatever force it might once have had; and now everything centered around the possibility of a foreign alliance.

It was doubted by many that the colonies, if independent, could stick together. If one or two refused to go into the confederation (and—*what* confederation? *what* after all had been organized?) or if, after entering, they dropped out, then the whole structure would collapse.

Even if they did stick together, and work together, a big "if," nobody supposed that they could stand alone as a separate nation. The need of some sort of European alliance was everywhere conceded. But wouldn't a patched-up arrangement with Great Britain be better than any sort of understanding, formal or otherwise, with either of the other nations mentioned in this connection—the rotten France of Louis XVI, the decadent and malodorous Spain of his cousin Charles III?

Would either Spain or France encourage the emergence of a vigorous new nation so near to their own remaining colonial possessions? Wouldn't they, rather, make a deal with England, swollen Albion, offering to withhold help from the colonies provided that certain lands were returned to them?

But assuming that it had to be France or Spain, why not sound those countries out in advance? We already had an agent, Silas Deane, in Paris, and we were probing sundry Spanish politicians. Why not wait until these men had reported?

Wait . . . wait . . .

Why not wait and see how the war came out? New York might be taken, true; but it couldn't last long. Great Britain—not to mention the colonies themselves!—simply could not afford a long war. If we were defeated in the conflict to come, it would go that such harder with us for having made an out-and-out statement of separation. On the other hand, if we were victorious, how much better to face the world declaring an independence we had already won?

Surely it was as clear to others as it was to us that we could not possibly stand alone; we must seek support. An avowal at this time might leave us frantically looking to right and left, above, below, before, behind, for possible allies. Wouldn't it be the part of wisdom to dicker first, to see what we could get, before we thus stripped ourselves naked?

The sun had gone away, though the heat continued, and horseflies buzzed as loudly as ever. Again and again the sky mumbled, and heat lightning flashed. It got so dark in the State House that candles were called for.

It was the charm of the committee-of-the-whole device that it permitted votes that would not be recorded, samplings that need not afterward be exposed. So it was this afternoon. After Dickinson had spoken the delegations were polled.

South Carolina was still opposed, as was Pennsylvania. The New York delegates did not vote. Delaware remained split, though the hawk-faced McKean insisted that Caesar Rodney would come, if only they'd wait.

It was Rutledge again who suggested that the committee of the whole request a postponement of the final vote—the Congressional vote—until the next day. He hinted, as he did so, that South Carolina might change its vote for the sake of unanimity, though the delegates did seeek a little more time to talk it over. John Dickinson sat silent.

The motion to postpone was carried. Ben Harrison stepped down, and John Hancock, after replacing the mace—he was punctilious about such matters—stepped up. Then the committee of the whole of the Second Continental Congress reported to the Second Continental Congress that it recommended that the debate be extended to the next day, a recommendation the Second Continental Congress adopted.

There was more business before it.

There was a motion to allot an aide-de-camp to a certain (unnamed) brigadier general. This was passed.

There was a motion to refer all the military letters read earlier in the day to the Board of War. This too was passed.

And finally there was still another letter from General Washington. This letter had just been placed upon the president's desk. It was read by the secretary. It was, as they had known it would be, about the desperate situation around New York City.

The Accounts communicated yesterday thro' Lieut. Davison's Letter are partly confirmed, and I dare say they will turn out to be true in the whole. For two or three days past three or four ships have been droping in and I just now received an Express from an Officer appointed to keep a look out on Staten Island, that forty five arrived to day, some say more, and I suppose the whole fleet will be within a day or two. I am hopeful before they are prepared to attack, that I shall get some reinforcements . . .

It struck a somber note, by no means dispelled by the low and bumbling sky.

The meeting was adjourned, the members rose—and as if this had been a signal there came, head-on, a frightful rain- and windstorm, howling maniacally. It might have been the end of the world.

Part Two: *July 2*

THIS METROPOLIS, "the happy, the peaceful, the elegant, the hospitable and polite city of Philadelphia," was one of the wonders for mankind to show. The steeple of Christ Church, where the bells were rung every Sunday and market day, was the tallest structure in town, and from it you could see clear across the city, vast though it was, extending a full mile along the river, from Vine Street to South Street, and westward for perhaps half a mile.

With a population of 38,000 it was the second largest city in the English-speaking world, larger than Bristol, larger than Dublin, behind only London itself. Moreover, this was not only a homogeneous population; it was a working one. A local newspaper recently had commented, a shade smugly perhaps, that half of the property in Philadelphia was owned by men who wore leather aprons, while most of the other half was owned by men whose fathers had. Where else but in America would that have been esteemed a boast?

It was wonderful in more ways than size, this city of brotherly love. It published books. It held a famous learned society. It was a port with a fabulously lush hinterland. Its streets were patrolled every night, probably the only city streets in the world of which this could be said. Many of those streets, too, were paved. The municipality even collected and disposed of garbage, and Philadelphia in consequence was breath-takingly clean, a model.

It was even cleaner than usual the morning of July 2, 1776, for there had been rain, off and on, throughout the night. It is unlikely that any sight-seers climbed to the steeple of Christ Church then. The sky loured, and the air was hot and close: at six o'clock, when some of the committees were about to sit, it was 70 degrees, and by the time that the Congress itself assembled at the State House it was 80.

* * * * *

There were letters. There were always letters.

There was one from George Washington, a faithful correspondent, with sundry enclosures—one from General Ward, one (seized) from Lieutenant Colonel Campbell to General Howe, one anonymous. These all pertained to military matters.

There was a letter from the council of the Massachusetts Bay Colony, and one from Governor Trumbull of Connecticut.

There was a letter from the paymaster-general, with a return of his weekly account.

The Washington letter was grave, even grim:

When I had the honor of addressing you Yesterday, I had only been informed of the arrival of Forty Five of the Fleet in the morning; since that I have received Authentic Intelligence from sundry persons, among them from General Greene, that one hundred and ten sail came in before Night, that they were counted, and that more were seen about dusk in the offing.

Soon after the session started it began to rain again, and the room was exceedingly stuffy, since it was necessary to close the windows entirely, even at the top.

It was ordered that the paymaster's weekly account be delivered to the Board of the Treasury, that the letter to General Howe be published, and that the rest of the letters be referred to the Board of War and Ordnance.

The rain grew worse, a downpour.

* * * * *

It was not of the weather that the members thought. In the immemorial manner of politicians they were counting noses.

Caesar Rodney had not put in an appearance to tip the Delaware scales to independence. They all knew him: he had been serving in Congress since the beginning, two years ago, and his was hardly a face and figure that anybody would forget.

Delaware was the next-to-the-smallest colony in size, just ahead of Rhode Island, and next-to-the-smallest in population

July 4, 1776

as well, being barely ahead of Georgia; yet it had a whole vote, like each of the others.

More important was Pennsylvania, the keystone; and it was immediately noted that two of Pennsylvania's most prominent and most conservative delegates were absent—Robert Morris and the redoubtable John Dickinson.

This was not a day to be absent, nor were they that sort of man, the conscientious Quaker and the shrewdest, most prosperous merchant in Philadelphia. Punctuality was habitual with them, a matter of personal pride. Dickinson, who was a member of many committees, took part in every debate on the floor, howsoever brief, howsoever petty. Morris seldom said anything, but he was always there—and on time.

Unless these two showed up before the committee of the whole was convened again, the Pennsylvania representation was cut to five. Three, either way, would commit the colony. Franklin's stand everybody knew. After his exertions in England he could never be for anything less than full and immediate independence. Judge Morton sat silent, a little apart from Humphries and Willing, who eyed him askance. *They* were die-hards, but they could no longer count upon his vote. James Wilson, eyeglasses low on his nose, was listening to Ben Franklin, who, leaning close, whispering earnestly, was making use of every moment before the fall of the gavel. Wilson looked entranced, entoiled. Franklin was sometimes called the most persuasive man in America.

Were there others to come? Why wasn't the meeting started?

It is not likely that any of these statesmen did anything so vulgar as look out of a window, but it is impossible to believe that their ears weren't cocked.

The State House, together with certain separate wooden sheds, stood in the middle of a large yard that for all intents and purposes was public, though it happened to be enclosed by a stone wall seven feet high. There was only one gateway cut into that wall, in the middle of the Walnut Street side, but though the gates were stout they were seldom if ever closed, so that people passed in and out at all hours. The State House in truth was a sort of central plaza or commons for Philadelphia, the scene of all manner or formal and informal gatherings or rallies, the place to which an overflow meeting indoors—say, in the long-room of the City Tavern on Second Street just above Walnut—would adjourn. It was for this reason that the Congressmen had to protect the sanctity of their squabbles by keeping the lower windows closed even in clear weather.

The yard was not paved. No attempt had been made to landscape or decorate it in any way, though it did contain a large and rather haphazard collection of old iron cannons, already obsolete, which seemed to have been dumped there less for their ornamental value than because nobody could think of anything else to do with them. It also contained, about forty feet north of the east wing, a small wooden platform erected by the American Philosophical Society for the purpose of observing the transit of Venus across the sun, June 3, 1769, and despite many squawks never torn down. This platform was often used by stump speakers.

There was no grass in the yard, and in dry weather, trampled as the earth was, a horse crossing it could easily be heard indoors. Such was not the case the rainy morning of July 2, 1776. Nevertheless there were cobbles in Walnut Street just outside the gate, and voices were pitched low while all ears were strained for the sound of hooves there.

When that sound did come, they rose as one man. McKean scurried outside, and a moment later he returned leading his friend Caesar Rodney, who with his vote would put Delaware into the independence column.

Rodney was described as: "the oddest looking man in the world; he is tall, thin and slender as a reed, pale; his face is not bigger than a large apple, yet there is sense and fire, spirit, wit and humor in his countenance." It was like the caustic John Adams to note that fire. Rodney, booted and spurred now, swaying with exhaustion, soaked, muddied, wore a green silk handkerchief over the left side of his face, which was eaten away by cancer.

Caesar Rodney was well-to-do, and a bachelor. He might have

gone to England, where he could have commanded such medical and surgical attention as would at least have eased his agony. He had been advised to do this, and had been considering it. But he could never go to England now—not after voting for the independence of the American colonies. He knew this. Everybody knew it.

Emaciated, he looked like a man who was dying. His doctor said that he was. Yet he had ridden all night over muddy roads, most of the time in rain, eighty miles from Dover, pushing his horse to the utmost in order to get there on time.

And he did get there on time.[21]

* * * * *

The rain grew ever worse. But the door was not opened, and there issued no sound from the cobblestones beyond the gate; and at last it grew clear to everyone, even the most patient, the fairest of mind, that John Dickinson and Robert Morris were not coming. Unlike William the Silent, they would not fight in the last ditch, though admittedly they had fought right up *to* it. But they had quit. They were staying away.

There were no bickerings at that session, and there was no discussion. Voices were not raised as the change into a committee of the whole was effected, as the vote was polled colony after colony.

It didn't take long.

First, the memorable resolutions, as originally introduced by Richard Henry Lee, which Mr. Thompson the clerk would read again:

Resolved, That these United Colonies are, and of right ought to be, free and independent States, that they are absolved from all allegiance to the British Crown, and that all political connection betwen them and the State of Great Britain is, and ought to be, totally dissolved.

That it is expedient forthwith to take the most effectual measures for forming foreign alliances.

That a plan of confederation be prepared and transmitted to the respective Colonies for their consideration and approbation.

Then they voted, group after group declaring itself in favor of independence, with the single exception of New York, whose delegates announced that they were *personally* in favor of the Lee resolutions, promising that as soon as their instructions were modified—which would be done any day now—they would vote with the others.

Delaware approved the resolutions. South Carolina was unanimous for them, now. And Pennsylvania, being split three to two—Franklin, Morton, Wilson *for,* Humphries and Willing still stubbornly *against*—cast her vote for independence.

No one cheered, for this was a dignified assembly; but the thing had been done.

Benjamin Harrison and John Hancock exchanged seats once again; the mace was replaced; and the committee of the whole duly reported its recommendation to the Second Continental Congress, which accepted and adopted it.

Almost as soon as the polling had ceased the rain did so as well. Yet the skies were clouded and low, and it was very hot.

* * * * *

A resolution that followed met no block.

Independence forces at the time of the postponement of this vote, three weeks earlier, had obtained one significant concession—appointment of a committee to frame a declaration of independence *in case* the Lee resolutions eventually were passed. This had been done June 10. The committee consisted of Benjamin Franklin, John Adams, Thomas Jefferson, Robert R. Livingston and Roger Sherman.

Sherman, from Connecticut, was a former shoemaker who had dabbled with great success in real estate and had taught himself law. A man of middle age, old here, he was an insatiable worker, getting up at five o'clock every morning, serving on many major committees. He had gray-brown hair, which he wore very long, and he was awkward in his manner. Though a tiresome speaker—he was wont to hold his left wrist in his right hand, making no gestures as he teetered on his heels, and never varying the pitch of his voice—he had been from the beginning an independence advocate. There were smoother men in this group; there was none more staunch.

Livingston was much younger, still in his twenties. He was an arch-conservative, not an independence-lover at all, and assumedly had been put on this committee as a sop to the big-money, big-family New York set. In any event, he, like Roger Sherman, seems to have done little or nothing about it. If there was ever a meeting of this committee, no record of it remains.

Adams was a natural choice; to have omitted him would be to excite talk; and the same could be said of Franklin.

That a Virginian should be on the committee was no more than ordinary horse-sense politics. The first congressional president, Hancock's predecessor, Peyton Randolph, had recently died. Washington was in the field. Patrick Henry, who cried "Give me liberty or give me death!" had gone back to Williamsburg to become the first governor of a new state; moreover, even if he had been present he might not have consented to serve, for he was one of those who believed that independence should not be declared until an alliance had been made with either Spain or France. Acerbic Carter Braxton was comparatively new in Philadelphia, and though he would vote for it for the sake of unanimity he was not keen for independence at this time. George Wythe (rhymes with Smith), a worker in the cause, if conservative, was effective on the floor—but no penman. Richard Henry Lee must have been thought of, and more than once; but because of a certain inflexibility in his political past—an inflexibility, or implacability, that cast more credit on his personal sense of honor than on his discretion—he was not notably popular with his fellow delegates from Virginia; also, it was thought that Lee already had gathered enough glory when as senior member of his delegation he introduced the independence resolutions, which were far more vital than the mere formal declaration. So the choice fell to Thomas Jefferson.

Dr. Franklin was the oldest and easily the most distinguished person on this committee, and it seems likely that the others

Richard Henry Lee. *Engraving made from a painting by Chappel.*

proposed that he draw up the document. If they did, he promptly and emphatically declined. Franklin knew his own weakness, as he was to confess later. He never could have kept a straight face. Inevitably, if Ben Franklin framed the Declaration of Independence, it would have contained at least a sprinkling of quips, some of which might not be perceived until it was too late. Whatever Franklin wrote would be straked and streaked with humor and drollery—qualities, as he himself was quick to point out, that should have no place in such a monumental statement.

John Adams had surely done as much as anyone to bring it about, and *he* might have written the Declaration of Independence. Jefferson, with a younger man's deference, suggested that he do this. These two had been made into a sort of subcommittee charged with the task of putting the thought into words.

"I said I will not: You shall do it."

"Oh no! Why will you not? You ought to do it."

"I will not."

"Why?"

"Reasons enough."

"What can be your reasons?"

"Reason 1st You are a Virginian and Virginia ought to appear at the head of this business. Reason 2nd I am obnoxious, suspected and unpopular; You are very much otherwise. Reason 3d You can write ten times better than I can."

"Well," said Jefferson, "if you are decided I will do as well as I can."[22]

So Jefferson wrote it. He wrote it on a portable desk placed across his knees—a desk he himself had invented, and designed, and caused to be made by Ben Randall, at that time his landlord[23]—while seated in the room where he did all his writing, the parlor of his small furnished apartment on the second floor at Market and Seventh streets. He wrote carefully and well, though he wrote fast, as always.[24] He consulted no book,[25] though it is unbelievable that he did not, if only subconsciously, recall to mind the opening words of the Virginia bill of rights,

Two views of Jefferson's lap-desk. *Courtesy Smithsonian Institution.*

July 4, 1776

written by his friend George Mason of Gunsden, adopted the other day, and twice lately published in Philadelphia newspapers: "That all men are born equally free and independent and have certain inherent natural rights . . . among which are enjoyment of life, liberty . . . and pursuing and obtaining happiness and safety." If so, it was no wonder, and nothing for his enemies to gloat over, for he himself had written the preamble of that great document, the part from which the above lines were taken. Unfashionably he scorned to make any quotation, classical or otherwise, for it was not his function, as he saw it, to be a modern mouthpiece for Aristotle, Cicero, Grotius, Puffendorf, Locke, nor yet Burlamaqui, Beccaria, Montesquieu, Hooker, except as the reflections of these thinkers, all of whose works, well-thumbed, might be found in Carpenter's Hall down the street, had been strained through the minds of the members of the Continental Congress. There was no new thought in what he wrote, no idea that had not been expressed a hundred times in the past two years right here in the State House. Nor did he mean that there should be. He was playing not the prophet but the agent.

Jefferson's first rough draft:

When in the course of human events it becomes necessary for a people to advance from that subordination in which they have hitherto remained, & to assume among the powers of the earth the equal & independent station to which the laws of nature & of nature's god entitle them, a decent respect to the opinions of mankind requires that they should declare the causes which impel them to the change.

We hold these truths to be sacred & undeniable; that all men are created equal & independent, that from that equal creation they derive rights inherent & inalienable, among which are the preservation of life, & liberty, & the pursuit of happiness; that to secure these ends, governments are instituted among men, deriving their just powers from the consent of the governed; that whenever any form of government shall become destructive of these ends, it is the right of the people to alter or abolish it, & to institute new government, laying it's foundation on such principles & organizing it's powers in such form, as to them shall seem most likely to effect their safety & happiness. prudence indeed will dictate that governments long established should not be changed for light and transient causes: and accordingly all experience hath shewn that mankind are more disposed to suffer while evils are sufferable, than to right themselves by abolishing the forms to which they are accustomed. but when a long train of abuses & usurpations, begun at a distinguished period, & pursuing invariably the same object, evinces a design to subject them to arbitrary power, it is their right, it is their duty, to throw off such government & to provide new guards for their future security. such has been the patient sufferance of these colonies; & such is now the necessity which constrains them to expunge their former systems of government. the history of his present majesty, is a history of unremitting injuries and usurpations, among which no one fact stands single or solitary to contradict the uniform tenor of the rest, all of which have in direct object the establishment of an absolute tyranny over these states. to prove this, let facts be submitted to a candid world, for the truth of which we pledge a faith yet unsullied by falsehood.

he has refused his assent to laws the most wholesome and necessary for the public good:
he has forbidden his governors to pass laws of immediate & pressing importance, unless suspended in their operation till his assent should be obtained; and when so suspended, he has neglected utterly to attend to them.
he has refused to pass other laws for the accomodation of large districts of people unless those people would relinquish the right of representation, a right inestimable to them, & formidable to tyrants alone:
he has dissolved Representative houses repeatedly & continually, for opposing with manly firmness his invasions

July 4, 1776

on the rights of the people:

he has refused for a long space of time to cause others to be elected, whereby the legislative powers, incapable of annihilation, have returned to the people at large for their exercise, the state remaining in the mean time exposed to all the dangers of invasions from without, & convulsions within:

he has endeavored to prevent the population of these states; for that purpose obstructing the laws for naturalization of foreigners; refusing to pass others to encourage their migration hither; & raising the conditions of new appropriations of lands:

he has suffered the administration of justice totally to cease in some of these colonies, refusing his assent to laws for establishing judiciary powers:

he has made our judges dependant on his will alone, for the tenure of their offices, and amount of their salaries:

he has erected a multitude of new offices by a self-assumed power, & sent hither swarms of officers to harrass our people & eat out their substance;

he has kept among us in times of peace standing armies & ships of war:

he has affected to render the military, independent of & superior to the civil power:

he has combined with others to subject us to a jurisdiction foreign to our constitutions and unacknoleged by our laws; giving his assent to their pretended acts of legislation, for quartering large bodies of armed troops among us;

    for protecting them by a mock-trial from punishment for any murders they should commit on the inhabitants of these states;

    for cutting off our trade with all parts of the world;

    for imposing taxes on us without our consent;

    for depriving us of the benefits of trial by jury;

    for transporting us beyond seas to be tried for pretended offences:

for taking away our charters, & altering fundamentally the forms of our governments;

for suspending our own legislatures & declaring themselves invested with power to legislate for us in all cases whatsoever:

he has abdicated government here, withdrawing his governors, & declaring us out of his allegiance & protection:

he has plundered our seas, ravaged our coasts, burnt our towns & destroyed the lives of our people:

he is at this time transporting large armies of foreign mercenaries to compleat the works of death, desolation & tyranny, already begun with circumstances of cruelty & perfidy unworthy the head of a civilized nation:

he has endeavored to bring on the inhabitants of our frontiers the merciless Indian savages, whose known rule of warfare is an undistinguished destruction of all ages, sexes, & conditions of existence:

he has incited treasonable insurrections in our fellow-subjects, with the allurements of forfeiture & confiscation of our property:

he has waged cruel war against nature itself, violating it's most sacred rights of life & liberty in the persons of a distant people who never offended him, captivating & carrying them into slavery in another hemisphere, or to incur miserable death in their transportation thither. this piratical warfare, the opprobrium of *infidel* powers, is the warfare of the CHRISTIAN king of Great Britain. determined to keep open a market where MEN should be bought & sold, he has prostituted his negative for suppressing every legislative attempt to prohibit or to restrain this execrable commerce: and that this assemblage of horrors might want no fact of distinguished die, he is now exciting these very people to rise in arms among us, and to purchase that liberty of which *he* has deprived them, by murdering the people upon whim *he* also obtruded them; thus paying off former crimes committed against the *liberties* of one people, with crimes which he urges them to commit against the *lives* of another.

in every stage of these oppressions we have petitioned for redress in the most humble terms; our repeated petitions have been answered by repeated injury. a prince whose character is thus marked by every act which may define a tyrant, is unfit to be the ruler of a people who mean to be free. future ages will scarce believe that the hardiness of one man, adventured within the short compass of 12 years only, on so many acts of tyranny without a mask, over a people fostered & fixed in principles of liberty.

Nor have we been wanting in attentions to our British brethren. we have warned them from time to time of attempts by their legislature to extend a jurisdiction over these our states. we have reminded them of the circumstances of our emigration & settlement here, no one of which could warrant so strange a pretension: that these were effected at the expence of our own blood & treasure, unassisted by the wealth or the strength of Great Britain: that in constituting indeed our several forms of government, we had adopted one common king, thereby laying a foundation for perpetual league & amity with them: but that submission to their parliament was no part of our constitution, nor ever in idea, if history may be credited: and we appealed to their native justice & magnanimity, as well as to the ties of our common kindred to disavow these usurpations which were likely to interrupt our correspondence & connection. they too have been deaf to the voice of justice & of consanguinity, & when occasions have been given them, by the regular course of their laws, of removing from their councils the disturbers of our harmony, they have by their free election re-established them in power. at this very time too they are permitting their chief magistrate to send over not only soldiers of our common blood, but Scotch & foreign mercenaries to invade & deluge us in blood. these facts have given the last stab to agonizing affection, and manly spirit bids us to forget our former love for them, and to hold them as we hold the rest of mankind, enemies in war, in peace friends. we might have been a free & a great people together; but a communication of grandeur & of freedom it seems is below their dignity. be it so, since they will have it: the road to glory & happiness is open to us too; we will climb it in a separate state, and acquiesce in the necessity which pronounces our everlasting Adieu!

We therefore the representatives of the United States of America in General Congress assembled do, in the name & by the authority of the good people of these states, reject and renounce all allegiance & subjection to the kings of Great Britain & all others who may hereafter claim by, through, or under them; we utterly dissolve & break off all political connection which may have heretofore subsisted between us & the people or parliament of Great Britain; and finally we do assert and declare these colonies to be free and independent states, and that as free & independent states they shall hereafter have power to levy war, conclude peace, contract alliances, establish commerce, & to do all other acts and things which independent states may of right do. And for the support of this declaration we mutually pledge to each other our lives, our fortunes, & our sacred honour.[26]

Adams approved on the whole, though he did think that the author had been too harsh in his language when he referred to King George as a "tyrant." That might be all right for a hack like Tom Paine, but for a personage like Mr. Jefferson, who was declaiming for his fellow countrymen on a solemn occasion, it was, Adams thought, undignified and possibly even unfair. Adams also, while warmly in favor of the anti-slavery fulmination, doubted that the committee would ever get that "vehement philippic" through a Congress containing so many Southerners. However, Adams kept these misgivings to himself, endorsing the rough draft of the Declaration of Independence, which Jefferson thereupon showed to Benjamin Franklin.

Franklin too made a few small changes. These were not such as to canker an author's soul, any more than were the few slight changes made by Adams.

Then this piece of writing was submitted as a committee report to the Congress, where it was held on the table until such time as the Lee resolutions were passed, *if* they were.

Today, Tuesday, July 2, those resolutions had been passed, and the next natural order of business was to consider the proposed paper. But not immediately; for it was past the middle of the afternoon, and very hot and humid, and the horseflies were worse than ever.

A resolution was passed, with true unanimity: "That this Congress will, to morrow, again resolve itself into a committee of the whole, to take into their farther consideration the declaration of independence."

There was one more matter on the agenda for today, a matter of naval discipline, and a resolution was passed authorizing the Marine Committee to make an inquiry into the conduct of two certain officers.

The session then was adjourned until nine o'clock the next morning.

Thomas Jefferson always had been a sober man, but he must have been more than usually serious of mien when he went back to the Graaf house that evening. Victory had been won—for the cause, but not yet for the author. The next day, Wednesday, July 3, would tell the tale. The members of the Second Continental Congress were highly articulate men, often cantankerous, and they would cavil, each one thinking that he knew something about literary style and might himself have been a writer if he'd ever found the time. They would not be as gentle with the composition as Dr. Franklin had been, and Mr. Adams. It must have been a long night for Fred Graaf's boarder.

Part Three: *July 3*

It is sometimes said of George III that at least he was a good family man. This was no tradition in his house. The first George brought over from Germany not his wife (he kept *her* locked in a tower) but a couple of mattress-mates who were put in charge of patronage. These were known, from their figures, as the Elephant (Charlotte Sophia Kielmannsegge, whom he made Countess of Darlington) and the Beanpole (Ehrengard Melusina von Schulenburg, whom he made Duchess of Kendal). Though George I did not confine himself to these grizzly hucksters, he never did go to bed with an Englishwoman, possibly because of the language barrier: he had not troubled himself to learn the tongue of Shakespeare. His son, the Prince of Wales, was wedded to an extraordinary princess, much too good for him, Caroline of Anspach; and for a Hanoverian he was fairly faithful. Certainly he wept when she died. The choleric little man (George II by this time), blubbering, tears pouring down his cheeks, heard her beg him to remarry. *"Non, non!"* he cried. *"J'aurai des maîtresses!"* The poor dying woman sighed: *"Ah, mon Dieu, cela n'empêche pas!"*[27] *His* heir, the featherbrained Freddy, made out well, if swinishly, in many a bedroom back and forth across the land. But George III was a good family man. From the time that he was married—to an incredibly ugly princess—he never looked at another woman. He had fifteen children, all legitimate. This did not count against him in the American colonies, where infidelity was not the fashion.

The founders at Philadelphia had much to do; but they could write to their wives. Washington, Jefferson, Sam Adams, and many another, have left us masterpieces of marital correspondence, touching, throat-catching epistles; but the greatest of them all are the letters exchanged between John Adams and the incomparable Abigail.

A wife has been defined as a woman who sticks by a man through all the troubles he wouldn't have had if he had not married her. It was not so in the case of Abigail Adams, whose spouse would always have been in hot water anyway, having been born for it.

John Adams was called the Atlas of the independence movement and while many might admire him, and many fear him, none but his wife ever was likely to love this man. Short-tempered, somewhat short of stature too, he fought indefatigably, in committee as on the floor. To him a spade was never anything but a spade, and he refused to be reticent about it. He used to rise on his toes as he'd make some special point, and often he windmilled his arms as well. He was not one who suffered fools gladly—or in any other way. He didn't have the time. Besides sitting with the Congress five or six or seven hours a day, six days a week, he was in four years to serve on ninety committees, being chairman of twenty-four of these. Yet he could always manage to dash off a note to "dear Abbey."

His writing style was called "more energetic than elegant,"[28] and so it is; but it is also unexpectedly modern in sound, being peppered with phrases like "in the dumps," "a brown study," "there is some spunk in it." The prevailing note is one of impatience. John Adams was no man for halfway measures.

The morning of July 3, 1776, was a fine, clear, cool one, a morning of fresh north winds, hinting that the hot spell had been broken—hinting falsely, as it turned out. At six or so, before breakfast, John Adams, exuberant even at that hour, addressed himself to his beloved wife.

"Yesterday the greatest question was decided which ever was debated in America, and a greater perhaps never was nor will be decided among men . . ."

That was a mere note. Between committee meetings that same morning, he got an opportunity to write more at length:

> The second day of July, 1776, will be the most memorable epocha in the history of America. I am apt to believe

John Adams. *Engraving made from a painting by Chappel*

that it will be celebrated by succeeeding generations as the great Anniversary Festival. It ought to be commemorated as the day of deliverance, by solemn acts of devotion to God Almighty. It ought to be solemnized with pomp, and parade, with shows, games, sports, bells, bonfires, and illuminations, from one end of this continent to the other, from this time forward for evermore. You will think me transported with enthusiasm, but I am not. I am well aware of the toil and blood and treasure that it will cost us to maintain this Declaration, and support and defend these states. Yet through all the gloom I can see the rays of ravishing light and glory. I can see that the end is more than worth all the means; and that posterity will triumph in that day's transaction, even though we should rue it, which I trust in God we shall not.

Always impetuous, Adams here was jumping to yet another conclusion. The Declaration of Independence had not been passed, as he so exultantly told Abbey. It had been but introduced, and surely all day today, perhaps other days as well, would be spent in debating it—not debating its fate, which was fixed, but rather its wordage.

Although from John Adams' point of view it was all over but the shouting, Thomas Jefferson did not think so. His great instant, his *prueba,* was about to come. Shy, every inch the writer, for all the multiplicity of his other pursuits, he must have known that this day would be hell for him. But he wouldn't let himself stay away. Not that he meant to speak! He never did open his mouth in the State House. But it might look improper if he wasn't there.

Quaking, if outwardly calm, he took a seat alone in the back of the hall. As usual, he took notes during the speeches. He had his portable desk with him.

Many must have glanced at him with meaning, ruminative. One came over and sat beside him, and gave him a simple encouraging smile, a smile of understanding.

Benjamin Franklin could always find time for an act of kindness; and, being one, he knew how authors felt. At seventy the oldest person in this body, he had views that were among the most advanced. Yet his manner—he who had met three kings—was mild. It was said of the Duke of Newcastle, when he was prime minister, that he "loses half an hour every morning and runs after it during the rest of the day, without being able to overtake it." Most emphatically this would not have applied to Dr. Franklin, who, in appearance the most placid, must have been the busiest man in the land. He was postmaster-general of the United Colonies (his $1,000-a-year salary he made over to the relief of wounded soldiers), and until a few months ago he had been a member of the Pennsylvania State Assembly, as well as chairman of the Pennsylvania Committee of Safety. He served on many Congressional committees, helping to arrange for the manufacture of saltpeter, the importation of gunpowder, the printing of money, the designing of weapons and of fortifications, the mining of the colonial deposits of lead, the fostering of colonial trade, and sundry other matters. With Patrick Henry and James Wilson he was in command of relations with the Indians in the middle department. He was charged with investigating the cheapest and most practical way of making salt, an item the new nation sadly needed. He was the chairman, practically if not officially, of the foreign affairs committee, and it was to Dr. Franklin—philosopher, scientist, inventor, diplomat, businessman—that the secret but fully authorized French agent, Achard de Bonvouloir, arriving in Philadelphia the other day, had applied. Yet despite his age, Ben Franklin was forever being appointed to committees that took him out of town—to New York to confer on possible peace terms with Lord Howe, to Boston to confer on the needs of the army with Washington, down the Delaware to supervise the installation of the ship-blocks he himself had invented, to Montreal to try to find out why our attack on Canada was going so badly. He never failed to respond, and never failed to do his best, which was very good indeed.

There might have been those who disagreed with Dr. Franklin, but no one who knew him could help loving him.

He took no part in debates, and only now and then made a

Benjamin Franklin. *Painted about 1784, by Joseph Duplessis. Courtesy of the New York Historical Society, New York City.*

polite pretense of listening. For this was not his milieu, the floor. He was no chest-thumper, no thunderer. It was in the corridors, in the yard, and over tavern tables that he excelled. During the times of recess he would work mightily for the cause. Meanwhile he was doing his duty as a delegate. He should be here, and he was. When it seemed a little hard to keep his face turned toward the speaker of the moment, he would rest his chin or sometimes even his forehead upon the hands that were folded over the top of his walking stick. There were many who believed that Dr. Franklin dozed at those times, catching up with his sleep, though nobody ever had heard him snore.

That some of those who had never met him pictured this man as a mouther of prissy if profitable aphorisms is no doubt attributable to his editorship of *Poor Richard's Almanack*. But it should be pointed out that Franklin only *collected* those early-to-bed-early-to-rise sayings; he did not *write* them. He was out not to moralize but to make money, and this he did extremely well. Yet he never permitted money to make him. He kept to the end an outrageous sense of fun. He loved elaborate hoaxes. His wit was dry, the wit of understatement, but his advice could sting: he has written some of the most bawdy letters in the language.

Poor Richard might counsel moderation in all things, but Franklin, once he could afford it, liked to stay up late, preferably over a bottle. As much as any man, more than most, he liked to overeat. Even as he sat beside Thomas Jefferson in the State House this July morning in 1776 he was suffering from gout, a gourmand's affliction.

It might be mentioned too that Franklin had an illegitimate son, William, whom he acknowledged and who was, indeed, made governor of New Jersey as a result of Dr. Franklin's influence. William Franklin seems to have been a serious, unimaginative sort, the born officeholder. He and his father did not see eye to eye politically, and as the sage moved further and further to the left, the son waxed more and more loyal. "You, who are a thorough courtier," Dr. Franklin wrote him just before returning to America, "see everything with government eyes."

While Congress was in session the sage had made one last try at reconciliation, visiting his son in New Jersey, arguing with him; but the visit proved fruitless, and the break became final. Only the other day impatient patriots had closed in upon the Tory Governor Franklin, depriving him of his post.[29]

And now, as the session of July 3 was about to begin, Dr. Franklin placed a comforting, paternal hand on the young Virginian's knee; but for a long while he was silent.

* * * * *

There was a letter, dated May 21 (it came from Augusta, Georgia), setting forth the troubles of the commissioners of Indian affairs in the southern department, and listing their expenses. This was read and approved, and the expense account referred to the Board of Treasury.

There was a letter, dated only yesterday, from the New Jersey convention, or revolutionary governing body. It was urgent in tone and, having to do with the so-called Flying Camp, touched off a long debate.

No letter had been received from General Washington yet today, but there were plenty of unofficial reports of the gathering of the British in and just outside of New York harbor. This was not a feint! It seemed unlikely that Washington could save the city; the redcoats already were streaming ashore on Staten Island, which he'd stripped as best he could. What if, having seized New York, the Howes, with that enormous army at their command, and with complete control of the seas, should leave a holding force there and with the balance of the troops go by water to Philadelphia, or perhaps—for there was nothing to stop them—march straight across the Jerseys?

Not a man could be spared from the northern army, made up largely of New Englanders and New Yorkers, if Burgoyne was to be prevented from making his way down through the lakes and the Hudson, to join with Howe in cutting the colonies in half.

Neither could Washington spare a man: that was clear. He might have used three times as many as he had.[30] As for the

South, troops from so far away, together with their provisions, might take too long to get to the scene of action; and what was more, they were needed at Charleston, which Clinton had under siege.[31]

As early as April, when news of the evacuation of Boston had been confirmed, the Congress summoned the Continental Commander-in-Chief to Philadelphia for conference on the next move. It was believed that Howe and his army, great even before his reinforcements had arrived, would sail for Halifax, there to refit the soldiers and ships and to dump ashore the loyalist refugees. But a sudden swoop on New York or even Philadelphia itself was conceivable; and it was not until the middle of May that Washington, his intelligence at last complete, could venture the long cross-country trip. On Saturday, May 25, Congress had appointed a committee consisting of Harrison, Hewes, Middleton, Lyman Hall, Read, Tilghman, William Livingston, Whipple, Sherman, Hopkins, Robert Livingston, John Adams, Wilson, and Richard Henry Lee to confer with him and with Major General Gates and Brigadier General Mifflin, who also had been summoned.[32] It was this committee that on May 29 approved the plan for a Flying Camp, recommending that it be made up of 6,000 militiamen from Pennsylvania, 3,400 from Maryland, and 600 from Delaware, besides the New Jersey militia, and that it be established somewhere near Amboy, New Jersey (this was later changed to New Brunswick). Such an army, it was believed, could get to Philadelphia before the British if the British went by sea, or, if they went by land, could intercept them without causing Washington to break his own lines. The militiamen, for the duration of their service in this army, which was to be only until the end of September, were to be commanded by a Continental general and were to be paid the same as regular Continental soldiers, whose wage was the highest in history.[33] This plan, after a long meeting as the committee of the whole, Congress had accepted, Monday, June 3.

Today, July 3, the Congress after much discussion passed

three resolutions concerning the Flying Camp. The first two were largely hortative, aimed at stirring up the Middle Colonies. The third empowered Washington to appoint a commanding officer of the Flying Camp and also to "direct proper persons to supply the men with rations."[34]

* * * * *

The fact that no letter had been received today from General Washington caused some uneasiness, for the air was filled with wild rumors about the invasion, and New York was not far away.

At least the Congressmen knew what to expect in the way of foreigners. Because of messages George Merchant, an escaped prisoner, had smuggled into the country, the facts were plain at last, and had been published—first in the *Pennsylvania Gazette,* May 22, and later in other papers.

The mercenaries — "auxiliaries" was the official British Army designation—were found to be needed when it was proved that not nearly enough men could be obtained even from Scotland and Ireland, even by scraping the barrel elsewhere: that is, emptying the jails. For a time it had looked as though Catherine the Great (Horace Walpole's "Sister Kitty"), who had a perfectly good army just back from war, might agree to rent 20,000 Russians. Negotiations indeed had gone far— when Frederick of Prussia intervened with a few sour sardonic words, ending *that.* Next, the British government had tried to hire the Scotch Brigade, a crack Netherlands outfit made up of Dutchmen though still largely officered by Scots; but the States-General, themselves so lately in rebellion, had put a stop to this on purely moral grounds. The princelings of central Germany, however, were not so squeamish. They did not have to be summoned, but came of their own accord, regiments in their hands, as it were, greed loud in their eyes.

In addition, certain British regiments destined for America were permitted to recruit in Germany. There was no record of how many such recruits were raised, but probably it was not many, for as soon as the various dukes and princes and landgraves realized what a market they were missing, they forbade the practice and began to offer the cannon fodder themselves, naming high prices.

Besides all this, the Elector of Hanover (George III of Great Britain) graciously chartered to George III of Great Britain 2,355 Hanoverian troops to relieve five British regiments stationed at Minorca and Gibraltar, which regiments were then dispatched to the American colonies.[36]

News of the approaching foreigners and of the shameful transactions that had gone into their raising, had greatly helped the patriots' cause, so hot was the indignation it touched off. Yet it was a terrible thing to sit and wait. Congress had done what it could, appointing a secret committee which, among other things, planned to flood the foreigners' camps with literature, and for this reason had caused thousands of handbills to be printed in German, promising, more or less, the moon.[36]

But—how big was the whole army, mercenaries and British combined? It was known that Burgoyne, carrying out a side show, if a large one, had about 10,000 men, regulars, fully equipped, in Canada, in addition to the local auxiliaries and Indians. It was known that extraordinary preparations had been in progress all over England, and that the treasury was being unmercifully squeezed, the popular imagination scared: the price of consols had dropped five points in the first five months of 1776. How many would land at New York, and what would they do? It might have been better to hear even bad news from Washington than no news at all.[37]

* * * * *

And now, while the paper Mr. Jefferson had written lay all unread upon the clerk's desk, the Continental Congress with maddening deliberation took up another matter.

It was resolved that the Marine Committee be empowered to contract with shipwrights to go to Lake Champlain and build a fleet there, a fleet designed to keep the British in Canada, on extraordinary terms, which were carefully set forth.

These shipwrights, or marine carpenters, were to get $34\frac{2}{3}$ dollars a month, one month's pay to be given in advance; their tools and arms were to be valued; each should be allowed a ration and a half, plus one half-pint of rum, a day; and finally, this phenomenal pay should start from the day they signed articles and continue until they were discharged, with an allowance of one day's pay for every twenty miles between the place where they were discharged and their respective homes.

The reason for paying a shipwright seven times as much as a soldier was clear enough, now. The poorly supplied army of the north, upon which so many fond hopes had been pinned when it invaded Canada, had, by sickness, winter, and by the British and Indians too, been badly mauled. Dragging its sick with it, this army had retreated to the lake region between Canada and upper New York, relentlessly chased by the foe. Here at last it must make a stand, or the cause of the United Colonies was lost.

Lake Champlain was the key. The British were not woodsmen; but even if they had been woodsmen, in one summer—and it was not possible to campaign in that country in the winter—they never could have built roads through the wilderness over which to transport their supplies and artillery, all the while protecting themselves against Indian-style delaying tactics, and keeping open their lines of communication and supply. They knew this. On the other hand, the water route was eminently practical. Once over the rapids of the Richelieu, which flows into the St. Lawrence, once on the shores of Lake Champlain itself, shores thick with suitable timber, they could construct boats that would carry troops, guns, and all supplies, free from fear of ambush. Champlain itself, which extends a few miles into Canada, is 130 miles long, from $\frac{1}{4}$ to 11 miles in width, and everywhere navigable, and at its southern tip it connects with Lake George, another north-south aquatic highway, the southern end of which is within a few miles of the upper reaches of the Hudson. The only way such an advance could be stopped was with gunboats built on the spot, a fleet rising out of the forest. From a distance this was hard to understand, but Congress by this time did understand it, and was willing to pay any price for shipyard workers.

July 4, 1776

The reason the price was so high was equally evident. Nobody believed that the war would last long—how could it? how could either side afford to go on fighting?—and along the coast, especially in Connecticut, Rhode Island, and Massachusetts, there was a natural wish to make as much money as possible in the short time, by the simplest if not the safest method: privateering. Every shipyard in those parts was working night and day, and any sort of tub that could be coaxed into holding the seas for a week at a time was snatched off the ways as fast as it was finished. The men who built those vessels were treated like kings, and paid that way too. Why should they leave such lordly pickings and go deep into a terrible wilderness, a place of sickness and mosquitoes, and scalp-seeking Indians, not to mention the British themselves, to work for the government? Of course the pay was high. It had to be.

Congress, this day, met the demand, faced the emergency. But it took some talk.

Then there was another matter. It was resolved that Benjamin Franklin and James Wilson, two of the commissioners for Indian affairs in the middle department, be authorized to discharge the bills drawn by a Mr. Morgan on the commissioners of that department.

And at last Mr. Hancock stepped down, and Ben Harrison the jolly stepped up, and the committee of the whole was in being again, and Charles Thompson the secretary read the Declaration of Independence, after which the Congressmen got out their editorial tomahawks, causing Mr. Jefferson to wince.

Dr. Franklin took his hand away from Jefferson's knee, but leaned closer.

"I'll tell you a story," he said.

* * * * *

Jefferson was a conscientious worker, and his associates too were conscientious, so that even before the paper was submitted to Congress as a committee report, June 28, certain changes had been made. Some of these changes were Franklin's, some

Adams'. Most of them were made by the author himself, or at any rate in his own hand, though they might have been suggested by one of the others.

These changes for the most part were toward clarity and moderation. Thus "equal and independent" had become "separate and equal," "his Majesty" was changed to "the King of Great Britain," and "the change" to "the separation," while "from that equal creation they derive rights" came out at last "they are endowed by their creator with equal rights," surely an improvement.

They made for brevity as well. "No one fact stands single or solitary," a redundancy, was reduced to "appears no solitary fact"; "deluge us in blood" was made "destroy us," and "everlasting Adieu!" was straightened into "eternal separation," the exclamation point being dropped. "Subjects" became "citizens," "power" became "Despotism," "injury" was pluralized, and the cumbersome "advance from that subordination in which they have hitherto remained" was struck out, to be replaced by "dissolve the political bands which have connected them with another."

This much had been done, so to speak "at home," within the family. It was quite another matter when the Declaration was brought up on the floor.

No one tossed so much as a pitying glance at the author of the Declaration of Independence as he sat in the back of the hall that afternoon and listened to them, after due discussion, triumphantly alter "neglected utterly" to "utterly neglected," and "suffered" to "obstructed," and "these our states" to "us."

No one, that is, but his companion, the good gray scientist Ben Franklin. And Franklin told him about a hatter.

It seems that there was this man who sold hats, and his name was Thompson, and when he was about to open his shop he started to make himself a handsome sign. It said on it: "John Thompson, Hatter, makes and sells hats for ready money," and to emphasize the point there was also a picture of a hat. One of his friends came along and remarked that the word "hatter" was superfluous, so Thompson cut that out. Somebody else put

Facsimile of the original draft by Jefferson of the Declaration of Independence

mankind are more disposed to suffer while evils are sufferable, than to right themselves by abolishing the forms to which they are accustomed. but when a long train of abuses & usurpations [begun at a distinguished period] & pursuing invariably the same object, evinces a design to reduce them under absolute Despotism, it is their right, it is their duty, to throw off such government & to provide new guards for their future security. such has been the patient sufferance of these colonies & such is now the necessity which constrains them to [expunge] their former systems of government. the history of the present majesty is a history of unremitting injuries and usurpations, [among which appears no solitary fact to contra-dict the uniform tenor of the rest, all of which] have in direct object the establishment of an absolute tyranny over these states. let facts be submitted to a candid world [for the truth of which we pledge a faith yet unsullied by falsehood.]
he has refused his assent to laws the most wholesome and necessary for the public good:
he has forbidden his governors to pass laws of immediate & pressing importance, unless suspended in their operation till his assent should be obtained; and when so suspended, he has neglected utterly to attend to them
he has refused to pass other laws for the accomodation of large districts of people unless those people would relinquish the right of representation in the legislature, a right inestimable to them & formidable to tyrants only.

July 4, 1776

in the thought that the word "makes" had no business to be there, since the men who buy hats don't care who makes them, and it was a shop, not a factory, he wished to advertise; and "makes" went too. A third thought the reference to ready money unnecessary, since no one expected credit from him; and he agreed. This left only "John Thompson sells hats." Silly, said somebody else. Certainly he wouldn't *give* them away, would he?

And so it came about that all that was left of the sign was "John Thompson" and a picture of a hat, which did very well.

Though the teller's personality might have flavored it, at best this was not much of a story, and Thomas Jefferson had no trouble keeping his laughter down to a point where it would not disturb those assiduous alterationists, the members of Congress. Yet the impulse that had prompted the story was a kind one, and Jefferson was touched. For a few minutes, at least, he did not even writhe.

Then they started to hatchet out his favorite "he has" allegation, the one that had to do with the slave trade and slave uprisings. He had worked very hard on that paragraph, for the subject was close to his heart.

But it went. Not simply the "waged cruel war against human nature itself," the "prostituted," the "assemblage of horrors," but the whole purple paragraph, the longest as it was the most fiery of the charges against George III.

Jefferson, sitting there, trying not to look hurt, attributed this particular piece of erasure to an unholy union of southern and New England delegates, the former objecting because they lived with slavery, a condemnation of which could be thought a condemnation of themselves, the latter because so many now-respectable New England fortunes had been founded, at least in part, upon this very slave trade. No doubt he was right, to some extent. But there were men in that room, and many of them, who thought that the slave trade paragraph was too violent, in bad taste, and, worst of all, slightly ridiculous. To fling that in the king's face seemed to them to be carrying matters a little too far. There were plenty of good, strong, well-grounded charges against George III as it was, without dragging in slavery. So they voted for it to go; and go it did, *in toto,* without the utterance of so much as a sad good-by.

And there would be more. But not today. The middle of the afternoon, dinnertime, was at hand, and the body adopted a resolution—"That this Congress will, to morrow, resolve itself into a committee of the whole, to take into their further consideration, the Declaration."

"Adjourned to 9 o'Clock to Morrow," Charles Thompson wrote.

And they filed out.

Part Four: *July 4*

It was a glorious morning, the sun shining, wind from the southeast.

Up especially early, young Jefferson of Virginia found time at last to buy that new thermometer, for which he paid £3, 15s. He also bought seven pairs of gloves for Martha, his wife, who was ill at home.

The air was clearing when he made for the State House. It was not so hot as it had been—68 degrees at six o'clock, it had risen to 72.5 when Congress sat down—nor were the horseflies so bad.

Congress got to work promptly, taking up an emergency measure about which there was some discussion—though no dissension.

> Resolved: That an application be made to the committee of safety of Pennsylvania for a supply of flints for the troops at New York: and that the colony of Pennsylvania and Delaware[38] be requested to embody their militia for the flying camp, with all expedition, and to march them, without delay, to the city of Philadelphia.

This done, the Congress transformed itself into a committee of the whole and caused the Declaration of Independence to be read aloud once more, and resumed debate on it.

* * * * *

That is, they resumed what Thomas Jefferson called "their depredations." Silent, he settled into his seat.

They cut out the phrase "by a self-assumed power."

Unexpectedly—since most of the changes they made were deletions and aimed at toning the Declaration down—after the word "perfidy" they wrote in "scarcely paralleled in the most barbarous ages."

". . . were likely to " became "would inevitably."

Every time the word occurred, Jefferson had written "it's," meaning not the contraction of "it is" but the possessive pronoun. Again and again bustling Congressmen cut out that apostrophe. (These were not slips. Jefferson always had written it "it's," evidently having some stubborn reason of his own.)

The document didn't lack defenders, especially stout John Adams, who was on his feet repeatedly, despite his own belief that his voice and presence were distasteful to many of the delegates, a belief not altogether without foundation. Adams, in Jefferson's words, "was the pillar of it's (the Declaration's) support on the floor of Congress, it's ablest advocate and defender against the multifarious assaults it encountered." And again: "John Adams was our Colossus on the floor. He was not graceful nor elegant, nor remarkably fluent, but he came out occasionally with a power of thought and expression, that moved us from our seats."

Adams or no Adams, the cutting continued.

After "settlement here" they removed "no one of which . . . may be credited: and."

The word "climb" made way for "must tread" and then the "must" was eliminated, and then the whole sentence, and soon afterward virtually the whole paragraph, whilst Jefferson, without a sound, groaned.

". . . inherent and inalienable rights" came out "certain unalienable rights." (Who it was who changed *in*alienable to *un*alienable probably never will be known: it could have been Adams or Franklin, or Jefferson himself, or some member of Congress; the words were used interchangeably, a matter of personal taste.)

Jefferson's "to send over not only soldiers of our common blood, but Scotch & foreign mercenaries to invade and destroy us" went early, and quite properly. The wonder was that Franklin and Adams had let such an uncalled-for slur get by. Aside from the chance that it might anger Congressmen of Scottish birth or antecedents—James Wilson and Dr. Witherspoon, for instance, or McKean of Delaware, or young Thomas Nelson, Jr., son and heir of "Scotch Tom" Nelson—or those who had visited or studied in Scotland—Richard Stockton, Benjamin Rush—it was an egregious error, a very bull, to list the Highlanders with "foreign mercenaries."

The breakup of the clan system in the Scottish Highlands thirty years before, when the Young Pretender's forces had been smashed at Culloden, had resulted in a great deal of hardship in that part of the world, rugged enough at best. The Highlanders, wild though they were, barefooted savages, and crushed though they had been by the brutalities that followed the battle, and the proscription of their ancient badges and tartans, their very clothes and implements—for kilt and trews, sporran and claymore and skene dhu, alike were now forbidden by law—were getting hungry, and getting ugly too. The land itself couldn't support them, now that their chiefs were not permitted to do so, and blackmail, cattle raids, really were being put down. Unless something was done about it there would be another uprising in those remote glens, another pouring-down, not Stuart-inspired this time but spontaneous. It was then that somebody had thought of enlisting whole regiments of Highlanders, with their own designations, their own tartans, slogans, and all the rest. This, if it worked, would at once thin the population of the Highlands, become a safety valve for some of the patriotic fervor that no number of suppressive laws could ever fully stifle, and help build up the British Army, which badly needed building up, being short of manpower just at a time when the empire boundaries had been so enormously expanded by the success over France. At first it was feared that the Highlanders, though admittedly of high courage in combat, never could be disciplined, and might prove to be "more than men in victory, less than women in defeat," for the military mind was dominated by the example of Frederick the Great, and blind obedience was the only virtue a soldier need show. The Highlanders, as it happened, proved to be excellent troops, and the army took and trained as many of them as it could get.[39] There were Highlanders among those who were pushing the colonial invasion forces out of Canada, and Highlanders too among those who even now were coming ashore on Staten Island; but England and Scotland had been united as Great Britain since the Act of Union in 1707, and each Highlander, whatever his garb, was an integral part of the British Army, no more to be classed as a "foreign mercenary" than a Welshman would be, or for that matter a Cockney from London Town. Thomas Jefferson was made to know this.

* * * * *

Lank, long-legged, laconic, Mr. Jefferson sat with his desk on his knees, and as though he had been a man repeatedly stabbing himself in the heart, with a pen noted each change as it was authorized—by underlining, by bracketing, by writing in the margins. He did this on his rough draft, which became in consequence a much blotted paper, in places all but illegible.

"Expunge" was softened to "alter."

After "candid world" the somewhat smug asseveration "for the truth of which we pledge a faith yet unsullied by falsehood" was struck out.

Jefferson had mentioned Parliament only twice, but even these times were too many. The Declaration was not to be directed even remotely at a body from which the Continental Congress already had formally dissevered itself and the colonies.

Yet even the King was not to be clubbed too vigorously. As Adams had foreseen, Congress thought that the tall young Virginian had gone too far. Of George III, for instance, that "future ages will scarcely believe that the hardiness of one man adventured, within the short compass of twelve years only, to lay a foundation so broad and so undisguised for tyranny over a people fostered and fixed in principles of freedom" sounded, to say the least of it, exaggerated. So Congress cut this out too.

There was a current fad—it could scarcely be called a movement—for the reduction of capital letters. Capitalization had been overdone, and now there were many who swung to the other extreme, among these being Thomas Jefferson, who, however, could be supposed to have some deeper and more rational reason—perhaps something to do with democracy?—for this leaning. Here is a war that has been forgotten, but it raised a great deal of dust in its day, especially when the "new men" began spelling "God" and "Nature" with small letters, which was blasphemous, and refused even to capitalize place-names like Paris and Stockholm and Monagahena, which was silly. "This is an affectation below Voltaire," spluttered Lord Chesterfield, one of many. The presence of Thomas Jefferson in such company—he who was anything but a man of whim, a blind follower of the fashions—is hard to explain. Yet there he was. Not only in the Declaration but also in his letters he fought shy of the upper case, even starting sentences with small letters, a confusing trick. His critics on the floor of Congress elected to ignore this idiosyncrasy—as no doubt they took it to be—and capital letters soon proliferated in the Declaration of Independence, commencing most of the nouns and even many of the adjectives and adverbs as well. Nobody turned to Jefferson with a "by your leave—" They just went ahead and did it.

Equally difficult to understand in the writing of so careful a man—but it wasn't a slip, for he did it again and again in the Declaration, as he did in all his private writing—was Jefferson's use of "it's," not as a contraction of "it is" but as the third person singular genitive. The Congressmen, again, chose to ride over this foible, if foible it was, and apostrophes fell like rain. (The correctors were, however, spared another characteristic of the Jefferson style—"your's" when the singular was meant. He had found no occasion to use "your's" in the Declaration of Independence.)

As the day wore on, the air getting warmer, the Congressmen waxed more and more bold in their verbal forays. Toward the end they began cutting out not merely phrases but whole sentences, as it seemed to them—or some of them—that young Jefferson had been altogether too wordy. Thus it was that some of the author's best-beloved lines were cast into oblivion, while no doubt he squirmed. However, they did not here make many changes, only deletions.

Excision indeed made up the greatest part of their editing. After all, they were not stupid men; and they were practical, hardheaded. They tended to trim the high-flown, especially toward the end, where Jefferson had fairly soared; and they hacked away the verbose. They did a good job too, as a side-by-side comparison of the rough draft and the final draft will show.

A total of eighty-six changes had been made, more than three-quarters of them on the floor. Four hundred and eighty words had been eliminated, leaving 1,337.

And at last, after the better part of three full days of wrangling, the Declaration of Independence was put to a vote.

* * * * *

Here in this hall Patrick Henry had thundered that he was no longer a Virginian, sir, but an American, and it was upon entering this chamber that the ineffable Dr. Benjamin Rush, a Philadelphia wit, graduate of the college at Princeton, was to avow that the act made him feel himself "a citizen of America."

All of which was very well, but still in the matter of precedent the delegates could be as touchy as that many dowagers about to go in to dinner, and it had early been agreed, as still another unwritten law of Congress, that the roll should be called from the north south. It happened to be that way. It could as well have been the other way 'round, or alphabetically.

This meant that the first person to vote for the Declaration of Independence on July 4, 1776, was the senior member of the New Hampshire delegation.

Josiah Bartlett was forty-seven years old, and came originally from Massachusetts, more recently from Kingston, New Hampshire. Tall, careless of his appearance, he was a man of few words. At home he was a physician, a member of the colonial legislature, a justice of the peace, and a colonel of militia. At Philadelphia until recently, when he was joined by William Whipple, a Portsmouth merchant only a few months his junior, he had represented New Hampshire alone, and in consequence he was a member of every important standing committee. On the floor his activity was slight. He hated long-windedness.

So it went: Massachusetts, Rhode Island, Connecticut—

New York was skipped, since its delegates still were forbidden to vote for independence.

Pennsylvania held as on Tuesday, two days before.

New Jersey, Maryland, Delaware, Virginia, North Carolina, South Carolina—

Lyman Hall, a transplanted Connecticut Yankee, a Yale man, large, good-natured, once a minister, now a physician, but always the patriot, at fifty-two was the senior member of the Georgia delegation, and presumably he cast not only his own vote but those of his friends and fellow delegates—Button Gwinnett, the hot-tempered Savannah merchant, and the very small, very smart, self-made lawyer from Augusta, George Walton.

The secretary recorded this vote, then passed the paper to the president, John Hancock, who signed it and passed it back. The secretary himself then signed it, not as a delegate, for he was not one, but to attest the signature of the president of the Congress. And the thing had been done.

* * * * *

There were no trumpets blown. No one stood on his chair and cheered. The afternoon was waning, and with a full calendar of routine work on its hands the Congress had no thought of delay.

It was ordered that the Declaration be printed under the supervision of the committee that had been appointed to frame it, and that copies be sent to all the legislatures, assemblies, and committees of safety, and to the several commanding officers of the Continental Army, for proclamation.

Then Robert Morris and Joseph Hewes were ordered to hire Mr. Walker's vessel—for what purpose was not recorded but assumedly something to do with the defense of Philadelphia port, the fortification of the mouth of the Delaware. Hewes was a North Carolina merchant, middle-aged by the standards of the State House, and conservative in his manner.

Morris, the merchant, was back. He had absented himself July 2 when the vote on the Lee resolutions was taken, as had his confrere, John Dickinson. Dickinson had not returned. Morris had, though he thought that the decision for independence had been taken at "an improper time". He was vice-president of the Pennsylvania committee of safety (Franklin was the president) and a very busy man. Though he disapproved, he would be ruled by the majority, a course he took to be no more than decent: "I think that the individual who declines the service of his country because its councils are not conformable to his ideas, makes but a bad subject; a good one will follow, if he cannot lead."[40]

The military situation in Canada and the northern New York wilderness was bad enough, but the forces under the Howe brothers, being so much nearer, and of indefinite strength, struck an even greater awe to the hearts of the delegates; and when another letter from General Washington, dated the previous day, was read, there was a grim silence.

> Since I had the honor of addressing you and on the same day several Ships more arrived within the Hook; making the number that came in then, 110, and there remains no doubt of the whole of the Fleet from Hallifax being now here. Yesterday Evening 50 of them came into the Bay and Anchored on the Staten Island side. Their views I cannot precisely determine, but am extremely apprehensive, as a part of them only came, that they mean to surround the island and secure the whole stock upon it.
>
> Our reinforcements of Militia are but small yet . . .

It was then resolved that the delegates from New York, New Jersey, and Pennsylvania confer with the Philadelphia committee of safety about local defenses. Their expenses would be guaranteed.

It was resolved that the Secret Committee be instructed to order that the flints that belonged to the Continental Army and were presently stored in Rhode Island be delivered to General Washington at or near New York.

It was resolved that Henry Wisner be empowered to send a man to Orange County to get a sample of flint; and his expenses were authorized.

There was balloting for two more middle department commissioners for Indian affairs, and Jasper Yeates and John Mont-

July 4, 1776

gomery were elected. The Congress then instructed the two commissioners who were present, James Wilson and Benjamin Franklin, so to notify the new commissioners. It was agreed to postpone the filling of the vacancies on the Committee for Indian Affairs until the following day.

It was voted to empower the president to hire enother private secretary.

The flint situation was an extremely serious one—you can't wage a war if your guns won't go off—and was discussed, informally, at some length.

It was agreed to pay a courier who had brought some dispatches from Trenton across the river.

A "device for the seal of the United States of America"—this was the first time that title ever had been used on an official document—was then authorized; and a committee consisting of Benjamin Franklin, John Adams, and Thomas Jefferson was instructed to bring in such a device.

It was resolved that the Secret Committee be instructed to sell twenty-five pounds of powder to John Garrison, of North Carolina.

The meeting was then adjourned.

Part Five: *Afterward*

IT WOULD BE pleasant to believe that a certain member of the Declaration of Independence committee, the nation's most distinguished printer, personally supervised the setting of type that night in John Dunlap's shop. It *could* have happened so; but there are two reasons to think that it did not.

Dr. Franklin was not well. Gout and other ailments incidental to age had been troubling him. A few months before, with the brothers Carroll of Maryland, he had gone to Canada, an arduous journey, to learn for Congress what was the matter with our invasion; and the trip (he had not expected to return alive) had taken something out of him. He was begging off from all but the most imperative committee meetings and, though he still dearly loved good company, good food and wine, was abstaining from all social activity, intent as he was on conserving the strength that was to carry him on for almost fifteen years longer, through the full setting-up of the nation.

The other reason is that the job was so badly done.

In the late eighteenth century the rules for punctuation and capitalization were hardly firm, fixed; but such as they were, the original printed Declaration of Independence broke virtually all of them, failing at the same time to make up any of its own. It followed no custom or precedent, no sort of accepted style. Perhaps the light was bad? Certainly it was a rush job, and the copy must have been hard to read, repeatedly interlined as it had been. It would seem almost certain that no member of the committee took the Congress's charge literally and appeared at the print shop to oversee the job. Printers were capricious men in those days, not given to taking orders anyway, and John Dunlap seems to have been no exception.

Incidentally, the original copy was lost—whether by Dunlap or by Charles Thompson. What was pasted, by means of wafers, into the space reserved for it in the journal of the Second Continental Congress was one of the printed broadsheets. This could not be entitled a "unanimous declaration," as the wish had been, for New York still was missing. Instead, it was headed "A Declaration by the Representatives of the United States in General Congress Assembled."

It was sent north, east, south, and west, starting the very next morning, but roads being what they were, it was some time before the celebrations occurred. Even in Philadelphia, where the thing had originated, not until July 8 was it read in public, appropriate arrangements having taken that long. It was read by a member of the Philadelphia committee of safety, probably John Nixon, standing on that eyesore, the round, wooden astronomical-observation platform erected by the American Philosophical Society some years earlier in the State House yard, and was greeted with cheers and the ringing of bells, and despite the shortage of gunpowder many men fired off muskets or, those who had them, Kentucky rifles (which always had been made in Pennsylvania anyway, not Kentucky). Similar scenes were taking place that day in Easton and in Trenton, and the following evening at six o'clock George Washington had the Declaration read aloud to his lined-up troops in New York. It was a wild night, that night in Manhattan. Much to the disgust of the General, who thought it indecorous, many of the civilians, the so-called Sons of Liberty, rioted, smashing Tory fanlights and sidelights and hauling down the lead equestrian statue of King George in Bowling Green, a good part of which actually was used to make bullets, as promised—42,088 of them, at Litchfield, Connecticut.

And so it went. In centers of population and in militia camps all up and down the thirteen colonies there were bonfires, bell-ringings, and a great deal of huzzaing—though no fireworks, an extravagance unknown to the colonies then. Liberty poles were erected. Effigies of George III, Guy Fawkes fashion, were burned or hanged or buried. Ebullience was the order of the day. Even when the news reached Georgia—in the second week of August, by ship—celebrations were arranged, cannons were fired.

Undoubtedly many thousands of loyalists stayed home during these outbursts, taking care to keep away from windows; and some might even have sneered. Yet all the hubbub was not contrived. A great deal of it was spontaneous. Even making allowances for the men who used the proclamation as an excuse to get drunk and smash things, thus paying off grudges against loyal-minded neighbors, still there can be no doubt that to very large numbers of Americans the announcement filled a gulf, answered a gnawing need. The back-and-forthing was over with. We had declared ourselves. For better or for worse, we were in it. Many of the hats that were waved were ragged ones, and many of the heads beneath them were empty of any conception of what lay ahead, the horrors of what after all was a civil war. Nonetheless, *emotionally* America for the moment was satisfied. The hunger had been there.

That the Declaration was framed in deathless prose was not generally noted at the time. The sentences that brought the loudest hurrahs were not those that mentioned the equality of men, the duty to resist despotism, the establishment in the sight of God of thirteen independent and free states, but rather the ones that castigated King George. The message had fire: this they knew. It was for later generations to learn that it was a fire that would never die.

* * * * *

On the night of Tuesday, July 9, the same night that the Liberty Boys ran wild in New York City, the New York State convention, meeting some miles north of there in the courthouse at White Plains, found that Congress's reasons for declaring the colonies free were "cogent and conclusive," and at last voted to relieve the delegates of the anti-independence restriction. New instructions were written, to be dispatched the following morning. These were read aloud to the Continental Congress the morning of the fifteenth by no less a person than President Hancock, after which New York formally cast its vote for the Declaration of Independence.

Whereupon the title of that paper was changed to what it is now: "The Unanimous Declaration of the Thirteen United States of America."

It was probably at about this time that the proposal was made that all of the members sign the Declaration.

This had not been a Congressional practice. The gravest of state papers issued so far, by either the First or the Second Continental Congress, had been signed by the president, whether Peyton Randolph of Virginia or his successor John Hancock of Massachusetts, after which they were signed by the secretary in order to attest that signature, as indeed had been done in the case of the Declaration of Independence.

There is nothing in the record at least to suggest that anybody had a general signing in mind at the time of the July 1, 2, 3, and 4 debate. Perhaps the criminality of the deed—in the eyes of the British government—made the setting-down of names seem advisable, so that no one Congressman would appear more punishable than any other. It could be that they all realized that unanimity never had been more urgently needed, and agreed "out of doors" that it ought to be advertised. Or, conceivably, Thomas Jefferson had had something of the sort in mind ever since he wrote the last sentence of the Declaration, which would seem to imply the supplement of seals or signatures, or both.

In any event, Congress on the morning of July 19 resolved that "the Declaration passed on the 4th, be fairly engrossed on parchment . . . and that the same, when engrossed, be signed by every member of Congress."

The job was done, probably by Timothy Matlack, a Philadelphian who did that sort of work and who was known to members of Congress, having been at one time Charles Thompson's assistant.

August 2 all was ready, and everyone present signed the thing.

John Hancock signed first, and was supposed to have said as he did so that he would make his signature a big one, so that John Bull (or, some said, King George) wouldn't have to put his spectacles on to read it. This is possible. Hancock's signature always had been a large one, replete wtih curliques and underlinings, for this (to the delight of graphologists)[41] was the kind of man he was. His signature on the Declaration of Independence, however, is about 50 percent larger than his usual one. Whatever the truth, the tale has lived, and a John Hancock means one thing to an American today—a signature.

The others lined up, and old habit prevailed, for they signed by colonies, states now, beginning with New Hampshire and proceeding south to end with Georgia.

Making allowance for the conventions of historical, heroic art, in which nothing is ever dirty or creased and nobody ever needs a shave, the scene must have been very similar to that later painted by John Trumbull, the artistic Trumbull, son of the governor of Connecticut, brother of the commissary-general of the Continental Army—the picture that hangs on the wall of half the school principals' offices in the land. Trumbull of course did not paint it from life: no outsider ever was allowed in that chamber when Congress was in session. But he did visit the room, and he studied it, and most of the Congressmen, probably about three-quarters of them, posed for him, though often much later. His Thomas Jefferson, for instance, though Jefferson must always have looked older than he was, is hardly thirty-three here: in fact he was the new republic's ambassador to France when he sat for this portrait.[42]

* * * * *

There were fifty-six Signers of the Declaration of Independence, including the president but not including the secretary, who didn't sign the engrossed copy. Together they, or rather their descendants, make up perhaps the nearest thing we have in this country to a closed, a point-at-able aristocracy, roughly comparable to the descendants in England of those Normans who accompanied Duke William across the Channel and fought at Hastings.[43] Any family that has a Signer in it, however remotely, is inordinately proud of him. Any town that has the grave of one will point it out before the War Memorial.

Signership can't be taken away, and of course it can no longer be conferred. Moreover, each case has been authenticated. If even half of the sideboards, milking stools, candlesticks, and pewter porringers claimed to have come over on her did so, the *Mayflower* of 1620 must have been a very much bigger vessel than the 180-tonner that histories have described. The signing of the Declaration was cluttered with no such furniture. The Signers were much more widely scattered, came from more varied backgrounds, professed different religions, and in every other way were more representative than the Crossers.

The Signers, moreover, were a productive lot. They left behind them a great deal more than an imperishable document.

There is even an organization of Descendants of the Signers of the Declaration of Independence, founded July 4, 1907, with headquarters, appropriately, in Philadelphia. It has more than 450 adult members.

An impressive list could be made of those who were not in Philadelphia on that momentous July 4. The man in the street, asked how many Signers of the Declaration of Independence he can name, might manage to come out with George Washington and Patrick Henry, and perhaps as an afterthought Alexander Hamilton. Hamilton, of course, was in New York, still a student at King's College. Washington too was in New York, at the head of the Continental Army. Patrick Henry was in Virginia.

Here then are the names of the Signers, as they appear (though the names of the states do not) on the document itself:

New Hampshire
Josiah Bartlett
Wm. Whipple
Matthew Thornton
Massachusetts Bay
Saml. Adams
John Adams
Robt. Treat Paine
Elbridge Gerry
Rhode Island
Step. Hopkins
William Ellery
Connecticut
Roger Sherman
Saml. Huntington
Wm. Williams
Oliver Wolcott
New York
Wm. Floyd
Phil. Livingston
Frans. Lewis
Lewis Morris

July 4, 1776

New Jersey
Richd. Stockton
Jno. Witherspoon
Fras. Hopkinson
John Hart
Abra. Clark
Pennsylvania
Robt. Morris
Benjamin Rush
Benja. Franklin
John Morton
Geo. Clymer
Jas. Smith
Geo. Taylor
James Wilson
Geo. Ross
Delaware
Caesar Rodney
Geo. Read
Tho. M'Kean
Maryland
Samuel Chase
Wm. Paca

Thos. Stone
Charles Carroll of Carrollton
Virginia
George Wythe
Richard Henry Lee
Thos. Jefferson
Benja. Harrison
Thos. Nelson, jr.
Francis Lightfoot Lee
Carter Braxton
North Carolina
Wm. Hooper
Joseph Hewes
John Penn
South Carolina
Edward Rutledge
Thos. Heyward, junr.
Thomas Lynch, junr.
Arthur Middleton
Georgia
Button Gwinnett
Lyman Hall
Geo. Walton

* * * * *

It should be made clear that not every man who voted for the Declaration signed it, just as not every man who signed it had voted for it. Changes were always being made in Congress, and between July 4 and August 2 there were several of these, the most notable being that of the Pennsylvania delegation. Robert Morris signed it, though he had not voted for it. Franklin, Wilson, and Morton both voted for and signed it. All the others, Rush, Clymer, Smith, Taylor, and Ross, were newcomers, just elected to Congress the other day. They *would* have voted for it if they'd been given the chance; and they were more than willing, they were eager, to sign it.

It would have been an odd Declaration of Independence without the signature of Richard Henry Lee, the Virginia Cicero, who had done at least as much as any other man, even including Jefferson, to bring it about. And that signature is there. But it was placed there later. Lee was not present when the Declaration was voted, July 4, and had not even been in Philadelphia when the momentous vote on his own resolutions was taken, July 2, for he had gone back to Williamsburg several days before this.

Elbridge Gerry of Massachusetts, though present throughout the great debate, and an "aye" voter consistently, had to be away from Philadelphia on business August 2, but he arranged to sign it some time later, the exact date not being certain.

That zealous if vociferous worker for the cause, Sam Chase of Annapolis, also did his signing at a later date.

The reason John Dickinson's name is absent is not that he refused to sign, but that at the time of the signing he was no longer a delegate, having been replaced because of his "anti" stand. Fanatics kept calling him a Tory, and he continued to ignore this charge, being busy with his military duties. The British too ignored it when a little later they went out of their way to burn his lovely home, Fairhill.

George Read of Delaware voted against it, but he signed it.

Robert Livingston, though a member of the committee appointed to frame the paper, didn't sign—because, like Dickinson, he had subsequently been replaced.

Matthew Thornton, an Irish-born delegate from New Hampshire, was not even elected to Congress until September 12, and didn't take his seat until November 4; but he too signed.

Nor was even Thornton the last one, though he was the latest to be elected.

Thomas McKean certainly was there throughout the early July debate, and as certainly voted in favor of independence. However, for a reason we do not know—but it was probably ill health—his name was not on the Declaration at the time Thornton, the fifty-fifth Signer, signed. In December of 1776, fearing that the British were about to swoop upon Philadelphia, the

July 4, 1776

Continental Congress retreated by wagon to Baltimore, taking all of its papers, including the Declaration, with it. In Baltimore, where the Congress lingered for more than two months, it was decided to have another printing of the Declaration, this time complete with signatures; for until then, the names of the Signers, excepting that of John Hancock, theoretically at least had been secret. So the new edition was printed—and a much better job it was than the one John Dunlap had done—and it was broadcast. McKean's name was not on it. He must have signed, then, some time in 1777.

* * * * *

There were no large companies in the country then, and each of the Signers could be called, for practical purposes, a self-employed man, a man of independent means.

Only one, Samuel Adams, could possibly be called a professional politician, a man who had made a career of it, though all in fact at this period were devoting all of their time and energy to the task of running the government, and none was a tyro.

Something over half of them were lawyers. A more exact count would be inadvisable because of the difficulty in defining a lawyer then. Certainly the thirty-odd who might have so designated themselves were not all *practicing* lawyers. It was the fashion for the sons of wealthy families, especially the large planter families in the South, to go to England for a few years and study law at the Middle Temple. This was more than merely a matter of prestige. A knowledge of law, particularly property law, could be a good thing to have when they settled down to administer the huge and complicated estates they would inherit. The same was true of members of the big proprietorial families of New York. These men might be admitted to the bar but they would never open law offices. On the other hand, there might have been more Signers like little Abraham Clark of Elizabethtown, New Jersey, known as "the poor man's counsellor." It is believed that Clark did not have a law degree, and he was outspoken in his criticism of many who did have, but though he did not ordinarily argue in court he certainly practiced law, selling legal advice. Others, like Hopkins of Rhode Island and Morton of Pennsylvania, were or had been judges and were always addressed by this title; but they were not members of the bar.

There was only one composer — tiny, jumpy, fast-talking Francis Hopkinson of New Jersey, who was also a poet and a member of the bar. It was he who designed the United States flag.

There were four physicians among the Signers, though only one, Benjamin Rush of Philadelphia, could be called a *full-time* medical man, and Rush had not been in Congress on July 4.

There were two clergymen, Lyman Hall of Georgia, who however had recently quit the pulpit to practice medicine, and Jonathan Witherspoon.[44] Dr. Witherspoon, in addition, enjoyed the distinction of being the only college president in Congress.

* * * * *

Though the colonies were largely agricultural, there being almost no manufactures or mines, and towns being few and small, there were not many farmers in the Continental Congress. Here again there is a difficulty of definition. Members of the southern planter aristocracy, for instance, like the powerful Knickerbocker burghers, though the greater part of their income came from crops their land yielded, would hardly have been willing to list themselves as farmers, or even agriculturists.

An overwhelming majority of the Signers had been born in the colonies of English ancestry. Excepting only William Paca, whose family, of Italian origin, had been in Maryland for many generations, all had roots at least somewhere in the British Islands. Those few who had been born abroad—Matthew Thornton, George Taylor, and James Smith in Ireland, James Wilson and Dr. Witherspoon in Scotland, Robert Morris and Button Gwinnett in England, Francis Lewis in Wales—with the exception of Dr. Witherspoon, a Johnny-come-lately, had been brought to these shores when very young. On the other hand, of the native sons not all had first known life in the same colony they were later to represent, this being particularly true of the faraway small colonies: for instance, none of the three New

Hampshire Signers was born in New Hampshire; none of the three Georgia Signers was born in Georgia.

* * * * *

The youngest Signer was Edward Rutledge, twenty-six and a half, and another South Carolinian only a few months older (just turned twenty-seven), Thomas Lynch, Jr., was the next-to-youngest. Young Lynch's father was in poor health, and the son had been sent to Philadelphia with him, partly as a nurse-companion; but the son was a full-fledged delegate from South Carolina, a whole Congressman, and he signed the Declaration, something his father, who had recently suffered a paralytic stroke, couldn't do. Lynch, Sr., could not be moved from Philadelphia, and he died there in December of that historic year. The son, as it turned out, was not only the next-to-youngest Signer but also the *shortest-lived* of them, for he died three years later when only thirty. He had just married, and with his bride was on his way to the West Indies to look over some property, when the ship went down at sea.

The oldest Signer (and by all odds the most entertaining) was Benjamin Franklin, who lived to be eighty-four. To a clergyman who just before his death wrote to ask him to define his religious beliefs, Franklin blandly answered that he no longer cared to trouble about these, since he would so soon be finding out for himself.

The second-to-oldest was Stephen Hopkins, the sage of Providence, Rhode Island, a man of moderate means and moderate habits, and of very little formal education, though well read. He was the first Chancellor of Rhode Island College, a former chief justice of the state, and nine times its governor. He was seventy at the time of the signing, only a few months younger than Franklin. He didn't drink much, but he loved to sit up talking, and he'd do that all night if he could get anybody to sit up with him. His signature is easily the wobbliest on the document, and it has sometimes been said that his hand shook like that because he was afraid of the punishment he might be incurring. This is nonsense, and no one would have dared to say it in old Judge Hopkins' presence. His neck indeed had been in a noose for many years, since again and again in his official acts he had taken the patriotic side. The truth is that on August 2, 1776, he was suffering from an ague.

The first of the Signers to die was John Morton, who passed away quietly in Chester in April, 1777, and is buried in St. James Church graveyard there.

Before the first year was out Button Gwinnett too died, though much more noisily. Back in Georgia in April, 1777, he was serving as acting governor when a brigadier named Lachlan McIntosh called him a scoundrel and a liar—and Gwinnett did the accepted thing. He winged McIntosh, who however lived. Gwinnett himself, squarely hit, survived for only a few days. He left his affairs in a mess, and very few of his autographs have survived; their scarcity makes them the most valuable of all. The latest to be sold fetched $50,000.[45]

No Quaker signed, though Quakers had worked to bring the thing about, and at least one Signer, Joseph Hewes of North Carolina, came of Quaker stock. No Jew signed. The only Roman Catholic was Charles Carroll of Carrollton, who was distinctive in other ways as well. He was of Irish extraction, the name having once been O'Carroll. He was the richest man in America, and since his inherited fortune has been estimated at £200,000 he could be called the nation's first millionaire. Though not elected to Congress until the very day the Declaration was adopted, July 4, 1776, he had long been identified with the patriot cause, in the Maryland assembly as well as in semi-official bodies. For instance, with Benjamin Franklin he and his brother John Carroll, a priest who was later to become the first Roman Catholic bishop in the United States, comprised the Canadian field investigating committee, the brothers having been picked in part because of their religion, in part because of their knowledge of French: they had been educatd in France and England.

It was sometimes said that Charles Carroll at the time of the signing had added "of Carrollton" to his name because he thought to protect a relative who, in the event of an American defeat, might suffer in his stead for this act of treason. This was not true. For many years he had been signing himself that way, ever since he came back from abroad, using the name of his principal though not his favorite estate, at first in order to distinguish himself from his father, Charles Carroll of Annapolis, later to distinguish himself from a cousin of the same name.

Charles Carroll of Carrollton was thirty-nine when he signed, somewhat above the mean average, yet he outlived all of the others, and when he died in 1832 at the age of ninety-four at his beloved Doughoregan Manor, near Ellicott City, Maryland, he was the last survivor of the fifty-six.

Finally, more than any other Signer, Charles Carroll of Carrollton bridged the gap between the old life and the new when, four years before his death, he formally opened the Baltimore & Ohio Railroad. It is probable, almost certain, that he was the only Signer who had even seen a steam locomotive.

* * * * *

Section I, Article III, of the constitution of the Descendants of the Signers of the Declaration of Independence provides that "Any lineal descendant of a Signer . . . twenty-one years of age or over, and possessing good moral character, shall be eligible to full membership of the society." The 1956 list, the latest available, contains the names of 458 adult members. A few of these, but very few, claim descent from two Signers: none claims descent from more than two. The Signer most often named, amazingly, is John Hart, a respected but inconspicuous New Jersey farmer, who took his seat in Congress only a few days before the beginning of the great debate, who made no speech, served on no important committee, and had done nothing notable before the signing, as he was to do nothing notable afterward. Sixty-one members claim descent from John Hart, as compared with 37 from Carter Braxton of Virginia, a pronounced Anglophile who believed that the very thought of independence was a snare and a delusion, and didn't mind saying so, a man who signed only because he took it to be his duty as an outnumbered delegate, and who later, because of his loyalist attitude, was not returned to Congress.

Judge Morton, who switched at the last moment, has 32

descendants in this group. Oliver Wolcott of Connecticut, who was for independence all the time, has 23; Robert Morris, who was against it, has 22, as has the redoubtable Richard Henry Lee. Ben Franklin has 21, Thomas Jefferson only 12. The obscure William Floyd of New York has 9 enrolled descendants, the same as the sensational Sam Adams; but John Adams has only one.

Mention has been made of the next-to-youngest Signer, Thomas Lynch, Jr., of South Carolina, who soon after his marriage—and less than three years after signing—went to sea with his bride in a ship that never was seen again. His name of course does not appear in the DSDI membership list.

It is understandable too that nobody claims descent from Caesar Rodney or Joseph Hewes, for these men were lifelong bachelors, the only ones among the fifty-six, Rodney because of his cancer, Hewes because of a sentimental vow to a maiden who died before he could marry her.

Samuel Huntington, George Wythe (rhymes with "Smith"), and Francis Lightfoot Lee, though married, were childless. James Wilson's one child died in infancy, like William Whipple's; and John Hancock's son and daughter did not survive childhood. But what has become of the descendants of Lyman Hall, who had a son; George Walton, who had two; William Williams and William Hooper, each of whom had three; and of James Smith, who was survived by five children; Elbridge Gerry by seven, Robert Treat Paine ("the great objector") by eight, and Abraham Clark by ten? Perhaps they just aren't joiners.

Benjamin ("Falstaff") Harrison, the lusty, might have been expected to leave a large progeny; and he did, though only eleven of his descendants are DSDI members. Harrison shares with John Adams the distinction of having sired a future president. Harrison's son William Henry, the senior partner in the Tippecanoe-and-Tyler-too campaign of 1836, was the ninth man elected president of the United States. The oldest man ever to be elected, before or since, sixty-eight, he was also the first to die in office, and as such the first to try to teach the politicians lessons they haven't learned yet—that presidents aren't immortal, and that a man who is the opposite in every important political respect to a presidential candidate may not make the best vice-president. William Henry Harrison died of pneumonia April 4, 1841, exactly a month after his inauguration. He was Ben Harrison's third son, and only three years old at the time of the signing of the Declaration of Independence. The signing Harrison, however—and in this he was unique—was to have yet another direct descendant in that high office. His great-grandson was the Benjamin Harrison who was our twenty-third president, sandwiched between the two Grover Cleveland terms.

* * * * *

Jefferson tells us that he made a "fair copy" of his original draft and that this was the one formally submitted to the Second Continental Congress by the committee June 28, 1776.

The original draft itself, generally known as the Rough Draft, is very rough indeed, being scratched and scored and erased and blotted, what with inserts and crossings-out and the corrections written either by Jefferson himself or by Adams or Franklin, not to mention Jefferson's marginal and textual notes of the changes Congress later made, yet it has survived and is among the Jefferson papers permanently on display at the Library of Congress. It could hardly be called *the* Declaration of Independence, though it was surely the first putting-down of the words, being assembled from bits and scraps, notes now gone. *The* Declaration of Independence might be the piece of paper the delegates in Philadelphia actually voted for on that momentous Fourth of July—that is, the "fair copy."

What became of this nobody knows. It certainly went to the printer, and since it was an official paper it should have been returned; but it doesn't appear in the records. It might have been lost, or (this is possible) simply thrown away as a thing of no consequence, once the proofs had been checked. Again, it could just conceivably have been stolen by some fanatical souvenir seeker who later feared to confess his crime and exhibit his prize.

Nobody seemed to care much, at the time. It was the act itself, rather than any record of the act, that inspired Americans then, and the veneration for the instrument displayed everywhere today was not in evidence then, men being too busy. Nevertheless Congress clearly knew that it had done something of world-shaking importance, and when it voted, July 19, to have the Declaration engrossed on parchment it was taking a step new in its history.

As we have seen, most but not all of the signing was done August 2, and the Signers used different pens and—more telling —different inks. Ink does not sink into parchment as deeply as it does into paper, and when dried it is more easily chipped from the surface. For many years the Declaration was rolled scrollwise from the bottom up, which meant that the signatures got the most scuffing. Apparently it was shown to anybody who expressed any special interest, but it was not publicly exhibited.

On the twelfth of December, 1776, Congress adjourned, to reconvene eight days later in Baltimore, whence the Declaration was taken by wagon, and where it stayed for more than two months in the custody of the secretary. Then, fear of a British attack on Philadelphia having faded, it was taken back to that city.

In September, 1777, however, the British threat was real, and Congress, Declaration and all, moved first to Lancaster, Pennsylvania, later to York, where the Declaration spent almost a year in the courthouse. Then back to Philadelphia. In 1783 the Congress went traveling again, though for other reasons, and the Declaration, never on display, went to Annapolis and Princeton, and the following year to Trenton. In 1785 the government moved to New York, and the Declaration of Independence was for a time stored on the second floor of the old City Hall on Wall Street, recently remodeled into the Federal Building (the present sub-treasury, before which Washington was inaugurated). John Jay, besides being chief justice, was acting secretary of state of the new republic then, but when the appointed secretary of state, Thomas Jefferson, came back from his French mission and took office, his creation was put into his charge. He had it for about three years. It is believed that he moved it from the building at Wall and Broad to his own temporary offices in lower Broadway.

At the end of 1790 the whole outfit moved back to Philadelphia, the nearest thing to a home that this document knew, though even there it was not lodged in the State House, still so called, but first at Market and Arch, later at Fifth and Chestnut.

The wilderness-fringed mud flats that were the new federal city of Washington were occupied in 1800, and the Declaration was lodged in the nearest thing to a fireproof building the place provided—the treasury at 19th Street and Pennsylvania Avenue. A few months later it was moved to the War Office Building on 17th Street, and there it remained until the summer of 1814, when British troops were converging upon the capital. To save it, the secretary of state, James Monroe, ordered it evacuated. It was put into a linen bag and carried by wagon to an old barn owned by one Edgar Patterson, two miles above Chain Bridge. It spent only a single night there, and then was taken to the Leesburg, Virginia, home of the Rev. Mr. Littlejohn, where it was kept for several weeks until the British had withdrawn not only their troops but their warships, when it went back to 17th Street.

Twice it was copied by expert penmen, and the copies engraved, proving a great commercial success; but this did not in any way damage the Declaration itself.

Secretary of State John Quincy Adams in 1823 ordered a facsimile made. This involved "lifting" a copy of the document, as a detective today lifts a dusted fingerprint. It was a wet process and one that, in the opinion of many later experts, cost the parchment a good part of its ink, especially the looser ink of the signatures.

When Daniel Webster was secretary of state in 1841 he decided that the Declaration should be put on public view, and he caused it to be mounted, framed, and moved to a place that was considered the latest word in fireproofing, the Patent Office at 7th & F streets. The Patent Office was at that time part of the Department of State. The Declaration shared a large frame with George Washington's commission as commander-in-chief of the Continental Army, and it was hung in a second floor hall opposite a window, so that sunlight beat upon it for many hours at a time, doing it no good.

It stayed there for thirty-five years, and when at the end of that time it was lent to Philadelphia for a centennial celebration (1876), it was found to be in bad shape—cracked, warped, the lettering faint, the signatures all but indistinguishable, some of them no more than cloudy blurs.

It was made much of in Philadelphia, naturally. Richard Henry Lee, a grandson of the original sponsor, read it to a huge crowd, after which it was placed under glass in a special safe, away from direct light, where it was viewed, probably, by more persons than had even seen it until this time.

Philadelphia, titillated by physical possession again, made most strenuous efforts to keep the Declaration of Independence, but the federal government would not let it go. However, its sorry appearance excited much talk, a near-scandal, and soon after it was returned to Washington, Congress by joint resolution empowered the secretary of the interior, the secretary of the Smithsonian Institution, and the librarian of Congress as a commission to study means of restoring it, the interior department to pay for the work (the Patent Office had lately been taken away from the Department of State and given to the new Department of the Interior, and by some queer chemico-political process which no one disputed, the Declaration of Independence went along with the building). Nothing was done about this resolution.

When State moved to the enormous new building it was to share with War and Navy, an *absolutely* fireproof structure, March 5, 1877, Interior gave the Declaration back. A few months later the Patent Office was burned to the ground.

May 5, 1880, almost four years after it had been authorized, the Interior-Smithsonian-Library-of-Congress committee met for the first time—at the call of the Department of the Interior, which might have been supposed to be out of the matter now.

July 4, 1776

Raising the old colonial flag at Independence Hall, Philadelphia, to touch off the centennial Independence celebration, 1876. *From sketches by Harry Ogden.*

It asked the president of the National Academy of Sciences, William B. Rogers, to appoint a committee of experts to examine the Declaration. He did this, and the committee's report opposed any try at restoration by means of chemicals, recommending only that the parchment be kept in a dark and quiet place.

Thirteen years after this report had been brought in, the Declaration of Independence was taken out of its frame and put in the basement, in a flat steel case.

There it remained for some time. The Constitution was with it (indeed, these two were inextricably linked, now and henceforth, both in public mountings and in the popular imagination), and the Constitution, a sturdier article, and of course somewhat younger, was sometimes shown to visitors; but to get a peek at the Declaration of Independence it was necessary to have the personal permission of the secretary of state.

That office was finding the responsibility irksome. If ever anything went wrong—

John Hay in 1903 (April 14) appealed again to the National Academy of Sciences, and another committee of experts was appointed, examined the document, and reported much as the first one had done twenty-two years before: no chemicals, no exhibition, no light.

April 21, 1920, Bainbridge Colby appointed yet another committee of experts, which reported May 5. This committee, unlike the others, thought that the Constitution and the Declaration alike might be exhibited provided that they were put between heavy panes of glass hermetically sealed. It criticized the fire arrangements the Department of State had made —or hadn't made—and specifically recommended that the two documents be transferred to the custody of the Library of Congress, where there were men who would know how to take care of them.

For some time nothing was done about this recommendation, and Colby passed from office with Wilson, Charles Evans Hughes coming in. On September 28, 1921, Secretary Hughes recommended to Warren Gamaliel Harding that the transfer

July 4, 1776 117

take place, and President Harding the very next day issued an executive order to this effect.

Having no precedent to guide him, Mr. Secretary Hughes simply sent word to Herbert Putnam, LL.D., librarian of Congress, that he had these two documents "when you are ready to receive them." Mr. Putnam drove right over to State in the nearest convenient vehicle, a mail truck belonging to the Library, and he took them back to his office, where he put them in a safe. This was the first automobile the Declaration of Independence ever had ridden in. It was a Model T Ford.

The Library did well by these charges, mounting them between double panes of glass with specially prepared gelatin to keep out actinic rays, and placing them in a bronze-and-marble "shrine" that was dedicated unostentatiously but very effectively February 28, 1924, by President Calvin Coolidge.

There they might still be, save for two things—World War II, and the opening of the National Archives Building.

As early as April 30, 1941, the librarian of Congress, the poet Archibald MacLeish, who had succeeded Mr. Putnam, was asking Secretary of the Treasury Morgenthau about the bullion depository at Fort Knox, and the secretary was promising him all the space he wanted—within reason.

December 23, 1941, both documents were removed from the glass-and-gelatin, and placed between two sheets of acid-free manila paper, in a container made of all-rag neutral millboard, where they were secured by Scotch tape. The whole thing then was put into a specially designed bronze container, which was heated for six hours at 90 degrees Fahrenheit in order to drive out all moisture. The day after Christmas—the attorney general having officially given it as his opinion that the act was legal—this container, sealed with wire and a lead seal, packed in rock wool, and placed in a heavy, metal-bound box 40 x 36 inches and weighing about 150 pounds, was carried with great secrecy to the Union Station and put into its own Pullman compartment on a train bound for Kentucky.

The arrangements, even in that time of high hysteria, suggested those that might have been made, say, in the Tower of

London if the crown jewels were about to be shifted to Paris for a little while. They are indicative of the changed attitude toward these two documents.

The compartments on either side were filled with Secret Service men, and more Secret Service men, not to mention a whole troop of soldiers, met the train at Louisville and escorted its precious cargo to the fort.[46]

In the years they spent at Fort Knox, the documents were several times unwrapped for examination by experts, who cleaned the Declaration, scraped its back, filled its cracks, plugged its holes. Truly, it got better attention in wartime than ever it had before.

When they were rewrapped, it was in Japanese tissue paper, and a piece of Japanese homemade paper impregnated with thymol was put in with them.

The military authorities having said that everything was safe now, on September 19, 1944, the Library of Congress took the documents back, and on October 1 of that year they were again made public in their "shrine," a guard of honor standing watch twenty-four hours a day.

The new National Archives Building was dedicated some years later, and it has a hall especially designed for the storage and exhibition of valuable papers. December 13, 1952, heavily escorted, the Declaration of Independence and the Constitution of the United States were taken to that building—a few blocks away—in an armored car.

On December 15, the rebuilt "shrine" was rededicated at a stupendous ceremony, the chief justice of the Supreme Court presiding, the President of the United States speaking.

* * * * *

The Declaration is enshrined, then, in the National Archives Building, where it is likely to stay; but in a larger sense it is enshrined in the hearts of its countrymen. There never was another parchment that meant so much to a people. The French Revolution produced no such state paper, nor the Russian.

Many years after the signing, a visitor to the home of the Marquis de Lafayette remarked upon an interesting exhibit—

a handsomely framed copperplate engraving of the original facsimile of the Declaration of Independence. One of the two hundred struck off in 1824, it had been presented to the nobleman by act of Congress. Beside it on the wall was an exactly similar frame containing nothing, a blank. "I am waiting for France to do the same," explained Lafayette.

Magna Carta (or Magna Charta, or the Great Charter) was no more than one of a series of such sets-of-concessions made by the Norman and Angevin kings to the barons of England, albeit the most important and most dramatic of these. It makes no general asseveration, and doesn't even attempt to sound a new note, being indeed in some ways reactionary, and concerned with the restoration of old rights rather than the achievement of new ones. It is a landmark in the history of the British constitution and so in the history of human liberty; but in itself, taken without relation to the events that preceded and followed it, it has almost no meaning at all. Its forestry provisions were so weak and so confused that the succeeding king was made to disgorge a separate charter devoted to them, two and a half years after Runnymede. Magna Carta does make a start toward certain great reforms—freedom of the church, cheap justice, limitation of military service, and protection from arbitrary arrest, and it even hints at trial by jury and the House of Commons, but the greatest part of it is devoted to protecting the large landowners against what they took to be excessive taxation. The lesser barons are remembered occasionally, the church rather less often, the merchant class hardly at all. The majority of the people of England at that time were serfs, or villeins, and these are mentioned only as property. Some of its clauses today sound almost incredibly petty. Chapter XXX, for example, forbids further commandeering of horses and carts for the royal service, as Chapter XXXI prohibits the seizure of firewood for the royal palaces. Chapter XXXIII insists upon the removal of all royal kydells or weirs, river nets that were thought to interfere with fishing. Chapter L demands the removal from office of sundry royal favorites, most of them foreigners, all of them mentioned by name. Magna Carta started as forty-eight baronial articles and ended some years later in the form of sixty-three chapters. Even in translation (the original was in medieval Latin) it is almost unreadable, as it is entirely unread.

The 1689 Declaration of Right and Bill of Rights as offered by the House of Commons to Mary and William of Orange as the price of the throne after James II had fled the land, and subsequently incorporated into law, are much more general documents. They were framed by a large committee, and the wording of them is commonplace to the point of painfulness, but they do state, succinctly and well, certain principles of English law that had never before been put on paper. They are noble in intent, but hardly exciting. They do not, like the Declaration of Independence, *announce* something; they do not *proclaim* something new. Invaluable though they proved to be to the British Constitution—still the English Constitution at the time—and to the American Constitution, when that came to be framed, they nevertheless are no more than a codification, a tracing-back of principles already established. They are a restating. Lawyers love them, and of course historians, but to the average man on either side of the sea the Bill of Rights is no more than a phrase, never a thing to stir the senses, to be taken into the heart, like the Declaration of Independence.

Hooker in his *Ecclesiastical Polity* appears to have been the first to put forth the consent-of-the-governed idea, but it was John Locke who made it his own, elucidating it in such a way that any man who read it would be convinced. Locke had a way of making the reader believe that he, the reader himself, had thought that very thing all the time. It was part of Locke's charm. It is also one of the reasons why he is no longer popular. He, as it were, painted himself out.

But Locke *was* read in his time, among others by young Thomas Jefferson, who never denied his influence. Men have complained that Jefferson "imitated" Locke. This is nonsense. Locke was no originator; he did not invent a system of philosophy or head a school of thought. He explained. He set forth. He summarized. It was not that he took the best thoughts of the best men of his time and made them his own; it was that the best thoughts of the best men of his time *were* his own thoughts, as indeed, for that matter, they were Jefferson's. Jefferson did not ape Locke; rather he echoed him, he reflected him, as no doubt he meant to do, for though he had a good opinion of his own literary skill he did not in this connection think of himself as an oracle, only as a mouthpiece.

One difference between Locke and Jefferson, an enormous one, is in the time. Locke was writing after the event, for the *Two Treatises of Government,* published in 1690, form in effect an *apology,* England's explanation and justification of the bloodless revolution of 1688, when the Stuart king, James II, was chased out, and a Hollander, William of Orange, asked in. When Jefferson wrote the Declaration, hostilities had been under way for more than a year, and though there had been no formal proclamation of a state of war—there never was to be—the world had been made to understand that the American colonies, or most of them, were committed to this conflict. The authority of Parliament had been repudiated, the King's troops fired upon, an army organized, a navy as well, and money issued, while negotiations for an alliance with the so-called mother country's mortal enemy had been opened. Nevertheless the Declaration of Independence was an *announcement*. This, as men everywhere knew, was *it.*

The prose of Locke's *Treatises* is sustained, even, smooth: "Chains are but an ill wearing, how much care soever hath been taken to file and polish them...." "The state of Nature has a law of Nature to govern it, which obliges every one, and reason, which is that law, teaches all mankind, who will but consult it, that being all equal and independent, no one ought to harm another in his life, health, liberty or possessions...." It flows like a great river, lovely to look at, massive, sure of itself. But the Declaration of Independence is a trumpet blast.

Locke proceeds with impeccable logic, never knowing a need to raise his voice; but Jefferson is righteously angry.

Who regards Locke today? A few scholars perhaps. The Declaration of Independence is read by millions, more all the time. The contempt that Publius Syrus tells us is bred of familiarity has never appeared in this case. Though it was crammed down our throats, yet have we savored it—and returned for more. Great portions of the American people have learned all or long parts of the Declaration of Independence, and not merely by memory but by heart, which is a different thing. The old lady who, having seen her first Shakespeare, said of *Hamlet* that it was an interesting play though it was a pity that it was all made up of quotations, might have said the same about the Declaration of Independence. Yet like *Hamlet* it remains good reading; and it always will be.

Interest in it grows. It is dramatic simply in its existence. In a world of ballyhoo it needs no ballyhoo. It stands alone, unmatched, unmatchable.

Nor is this chauvinism. There will always be cranks. Once in a blue moon a squeak of mockery might rise. Rufus Choate referred to the Declaration's "glittering and sounding generalities."[47] Santayana dismissed it as "a piece of literature, a salad of illusions."[48] Henry Mencken wrote a modern American version of it for the third edition of his *The American Language,* but it was not funny ("When things get so balled up that the people of a country have got to cut loose from some other country, and go it on their own hook, without asking permission from nobody . . . resolved . . . that we have throwed out the English King and don't want to have nothing to do with him no more, and are not taking no more English orders no more . . .") and he cut it out of the fourth edition, along with an equally sad burlesque of the Gettysburg Address.

The general voice, the chorus, in all lands and at all times, has been one of overwhelming approval. Many very great men, here and abroad, have made a habit of turning back to the Declaration of Independence from time to time, as to a cherished poem, and (though they know every word) reading it over again.

Not only do we love it: we are proud of it.

* * * * *

Cried Dr. Witherspoon's most distinguished successor:[49]

It is not a question of piety. We are not bound to adhere to the doctrines held by the signers of the Declaration of Independence: we are as free as they were to make and unmake governments. We are not here to worship men or a document. But neither are we here to indulge in mere rhetorical and uncritical eulogy. Every Fourth of July should be a time for examining our standards, our purposes, for determining afresh what principles and what forms of power we think most likely to effect our safety and happiness. That and that alone is the obligation the Declaration lays upon us. It is no fetish; its words lay no compulsion upon the thought of any free man, but it was drawn by men who thought, and it obliges those who receive its benefits to think likewise.

* * * * *

We have so long taken for granted the Glorious Fourth, with its fireworks and spread-eaglism, that it is hard to remember that other Independence days have been suggested.

Good Virginians have put forward May 15, the day when the new state government at Williamsburg formally voted to instruct Virginia's delegates to the Continental Congress to propose full independence for all of the American colonies—instructions that resulted directly and promptly in the famous Richard Henry Lee resolutions and in the Declaration of Independence itself.

On that day too, by coincidence, the statesmen in Philadelphia, after a bitter five-day debate, passed a resolution urging the various colonies to reorganize their governments along independent lines. The highly inflammable preamble to this resolution, written by John Adams, was a little Declaration of Independence in itself.

And on that same day the Virginia Declaration of Rights, written by George Mason of Gunston Hall, was adopted. This was published in the *Pennsylvania Evening Post* June 6 and the *Pennsylvania Gazette* June 12, and was undoubtedly read by Thomas Jefferson, who just then was preparing his masterpiece. Some of the phrases are strikingly similar:

> That all men are created by nature free and independent, and have certain inherent rights. . . . That all power is vested in, and consequently derived from, the people . . . whenever any government shall be found inadequate or contrary to these purposes, a majority of the community hath an indubitable, inalienable, and indefeasible right to reform, alter, or abolish it. . . .

There are those who contend that Jefferson's declaration was no more than an anticlimax.

John Adams thought that July 2, the day the independence resolutions actually were passed, "ought to be commemorated as the day of deliverance . . . solemnized with pomp, and parade, with shows, games, sports, bells, bonfires, and illuminations, from one end of this continent to the other, from this time forward forevermore."

Cases could be made for July 9 and July 15—the former the date when New York at last released its delegates from their anti-independence instructions; the latter the date when the Continental Congress was formally notified of this fact, making the thing unanimous, the date too when the embossing and signing were ordered.

Finally there will always be ancestor-worshippers who argue that August 2, the day of the signing, should be commemorated.

It doesn't matter now. Logic, history, have little enough to do with such decisions. To the public of the United States it always has been and always will be July 4.

* * * * *

The Declaration of Independence breaks into four parts. There is the preamble, which is brief, no more than a statement of intention. Then there is a long paragraph giving the philosophical reasons for the step to be taken. Then, making up the bulk of the thing, a series of charges against King George, the "he has's." And finally there is the actual declaration.

The preamble is what the schoolchild learns. It is a dignified statement, a proper opening, not stiff.

The second paragraph contains the real meat of the matter, setting forth *why*. This is the section most often subjected to dispute, dissenters from time to time pointing out, with a pathetic fervency, that all men are not created equal, neither are they endowed by their Creator with certain unalienable rights. Philosophy was the fashion in 1776, but when the Declaration first was published, and for some years thereafter, this paragraph seems to have caused little comment, one way or the other, it having been taken for granted that there would be a flowery and high-principled apologia before the real argument was introduced. The colonists were interested in more immediate matters. Philosophy was for the intellectual, an appropriate decoration but in itself without significance. The men on the street, or in the field, wanted sterner stuff, noisier, a specific hammer-and-tongs attack upon an actual physical being, namely King George.

Yet it is this very second paragraph that the world has come to love. To many Americans, indeed, it in itself *is* the Declaration of Independence.

The third part, the tirade, was greeted with whoops of joy —or howls of rage—when the Declaration was given to a waiting world. Here the author came right out with things, pulling no punches, naming names. This list of evils struck patriots of the time as the whole purpose of the Declaration, the rest being trim. Today it sounds choppy, even tending to be shrill. The injustices Jefferson set forth were largely local, scattered too, and it is hard for us to take them as seriously as he did. However, the charge that this is special pleading is an empty one. Of course it is special pleading! What else was it ever meant to be? To have conceded that there was another side to the question, to have conceded that there *was* a question, in the circumstances would have been preposterous. Yet truly this is the least of the four parts, the least exalted, and by far the longest. It is the part that the reader of today who is going to skip, skips.

And at last the close, the most magnificent curtain line in history:

"And for the support of this declaration, with a firm reliance on the protection of Divine Providence, we mutually pledge to each other our lives, our fortunes, and our sacred honour."

That said it. The world need never be in any doubt: this is America; it is where we stand.

Notes

Notes

1. It was torn down in 1883.

2. This despite the fact that the figure given embraces Vermont, a district then in dispute between New York and New Hampshire, and subsequently made into a separate state, the fourteenth. Sutherland, *Population Distribution in Colonial America.*

3. This was of course the present-day Independence Hall, little different then except in the matter of immediate surroundings. But the courthouse and the city hall had not yet been built.

4. Drake, *Tea Leaves,* etc., Intro. p. LXV.

5. No fewer than twenty-five pseudonyms have been traced to him. Davidson, *Propaganda and the American Revolution,* p. 5.

6. This might or might not have given us "caucus." The Caulkers' Club was a shipyards group with social-political proclivities in early eighteenth-century Boston, and this appears to be Webster's preference as an explanation of the word. The New English Dictionary (the Oxford) reports that Dr. J. H. Trumbull (*Proceedings of the American Philological Association,* 1872) points out that private clubs and in particular political clubs at that time (the Society of St. Tammany is an example) were fond of using Indian names. The Algonquin *caucauasu* (Captain John Smith, notoriously a poor speller, in *Virginia* has it *cawcawaassough*) meant one who urges or advises. Mencken (*American Language,* 4th ed., pp. 107-8) mentions this with approval but does not take sides. Neither do the compilers of the Smith-Zurcher *Dictionary of American Politics. The Dictionary of American English* lists a Boston newspaper quotation referring to a political meeting to be held in West *Corcus* in 1745, a possibility. The Matthews *Dic-*

tionary of Americanisms speaks well of the theory that the word referred to the conviviality of those early political meetings and comes from the late Greek *kavkos,* a cup, a theory the *Encyclopaedia Britannica* dismisses as "far-fetched." For many years the word was thought of as distinctively American, but in our own time the British have taken it up. They use it, however, only in its shady meaning of advanced political manipulation, skulduggery, and they have coined "caucusing" and "caucusdom," monstrosities unknown in the States.

7. *Historical and Political Reflections on the Rise and Proggress of the American Rebellion,* London, 1780. Galloway claimed that he had lost an estate valued at £40,000, leaving this behind. He was in small part reimbursed, and died in England.

8. Conway staunchly defended the colonies throughout the whole long wearisome conflict, and indeed it was he who, in 1782, formally proposed in Parliament that admission be made that America couldn't be whipped and that the war must end —a bitter pill but one that nevertheless was swallowed with an almost unseemly haste. But in 1776 Conway's power was negligible.

9. Years later when on a diplomatic errand to France John Adams was hailed as the great M. *Samuel* Adams, and it made him unhappy.

10. Gipson, *Coming of the Revolution,* p. 229.

11. Oberholtzer, *Robert Morris,* pp. 21-2; Stille, *John Dickinson,* p. 188.

12. He was to give our political vocabulary a word. After the war, and after a diplomatic flurry, Gerry became governor of Massachusetts. A pronounced Republican, he was opposed to the Federalist cause. In 1812 the Massachusetts senate, controlled by his followers, redistricted the state in such a way as to make their grip on it even more secure. This resulted in some oddly shaped voting areas, especially in Essex County, which suggested a certain animal. Gilbert Stuart, the portrait painter, happening to be in the office of Benjamin Russell, editor of the *Columbian Centinel,* saw this map on the wall.

Deftly he added a head, wings, claws. "That will do for a salamander," he said. "A Gerrymander!" cried Russell. *Memorial History of Boston,* Vol. III, p. 222. The details might have been fabricated for name-dropping purposes—Stuart was hardly likely to be hanging around newspaper offices—but something like this undoubtedly happened; and "gerrymander," "gerrymandering," and "to gerrymander" have stayed in the language.

13. In proportion to the population, this would be equivalent to today's 8,000,000, or about six times the sale *Gone With the Wind* had in its first year of publication. Mott, *Golden Multitudes,* p. 51. The first editions of *Common Sense* were signed "An Englishman," but this was dropped when its awkwardness became apparent. Tyler, *Literary History,* Vol. I, pp. 452-74. *Common Sense* quotations in this chapter and elsewhere in the book are taken, with the modernized spelling and capitalization, from Vol. II of the Centenary Memorial edition of *The Life and Writings of Thomas Paine,* edited by Daniel Edwin Wheeler. Adam Smith's *Wealth of Nations* was published that same year, but it did not make such a splash. The first volume of Gibbon's *Decline and Fall of the Roman Empire,* however, did.

14. Alexander, *A Revolutionary Conservative,* pp. 112-13.

15. Tyler calls this work "the most brilliant event in the literary history of the Revolution." *Literary History,* Vol. I, p. 234.

16. Rossiter, *Seedtime of the Republic,* p. 38.

17. Sweet, *Religion in Colonial America,* pp. 176-84.

18. Not until 1787 was an outside bishopric set up by the Church of England—in Nova Scotia. The second, the bishopric of Calcutta, was not established until 1814. Lecky, *History,* Vol. III, Chap. XII. Manross, *American Episcopal Church,* Chaps. 8, 9. Three groups were especially opposed to the creation of an American bishopric: the Whig politicians because they didn't want to see any more bishops in the House of Lords; the English and the colonial dissenters, and particularly the Congregationalists and the Presbyterians, because they

didn't want to see the Anglican Church get any stronger anywhere; and the churchmen at home because there was talk of an American bishop without any secular powers and they didn't want any such idea to spread. Manross, p. 156. At one time, when it seemed likely that a bishopric of New Jersey would be established, the seat to be Burlington, no less a person than Dean Swift began to organize his political influence for the purpose of getting the appointment. The creator of Lemuel Gulliver, however, dropped out of the scramble, horrified, when he learned that the bishop would be expected to *go* to New Jersey and even *live* there. He had supposed it to be a simple sinecure.

19. Of these, the Rev. Samuel Seabury, going on fifty at this time, a Yale man, born in Groton, Connecticut, was the most influential. His *Letters of a Westchester Farmer* ("The king of Great Britain was placed in the throne by virtue of an act of parliament; and he is king of America by virtue of being king of Great Britain. He is, therefore, king of America by act of parliament. And if we disclaim that authority of parliament which made him our king, we, in fact, reject him from being our king—for we disclaim that authority by which he is king at all.") were a sensation multitudinously answered, two of the answers being from an anonymous undergraduate at King's College (now Columbia) who later was identified as Alexander Hamilton. Seabury, persecuted, mauled, threw himself upon the mercy of the British in New York and was made chaplain of a loyalist regiment. The year the war ended he was elected bishop of Connecticut, but he could get no English bishop in England to consecrate him, none being willing to lay hands on a man who couldn't take the oath of allegiance. He at last persuaded three Scottish bishops to do it, and so became the first bishop of the Protestant Episcopal Church of the United States. Beardsley, *Seabury, passim;* Tyler, *Literary History,* Vol. I, pp. 249-55; Davidson, *Propaganda and the Revolution,* pp. 249-50-51; Manross, *American Episcopal Church,* p. 178. Spain was less stingy. At the end of the

eighteenth century there were in Latin America seven archbishops and forty-one bishops. Sweet, *Religion in America,* p. 66.

20. Charles Carroll of Carrollton, a devout Catholic, was one of the Signers, affixing his signature, like most of the others, August 2; but he was not present when independence was voted: he was not even elected to the Continental Congress until July 4.

21. He was forty-seven. A year before, when Paul Revere had made a ride of less than fifteen miles on good road on a chilly but bright, dry night, *he* was forty. Taylor, *Paul Revere,* pp. 130-67; Forbes, *Paul Revere,* pp. 251-70. Revere of course, while undeniably a staunch and efficient patriot, was only one of several express riders that night, and not the one who rode furthest and knocked on the most doors. It can be amusing to speculate on how much of a part his name—so cool, clean, brief, lacking in sibilants, easily pronounced, and with delightful alliterative possibilities—plays in his immortality. "Listen, my children, and you shall hear Of the midnight ride of William Dawes" simply wouldn't do.

22. Adams to Timothy Pickering, *Works,* Vol. II, p. 512.

23. This desk Jefferson years later gave to Joseph Coolidge, Jr., husband of his favorite granddaughter, Ellen Randolph, whose descendants in 1880 presented it to the federal government. It is now on permanent exhibition at the Library of Congress.

24. His output was prodigious. He *must* have written fast to write that much. The Lipscomb edition of his *Writings* runs to twenty fat volumes, while the new Boyd edition from Princeton, the *Papers,* is now up to only thirteen volumes but will eventually, the editors have announced, number at least fifty, probably more. The collected writings of John Adams, an indefatigable correspondent who lived to a ripe old age, fill ten fat volumes; those of his son fill seven. There are thirteen volumes of the *Public Papers and Addresses of Franklin D. Roosevelt* (Random House, Harper, Macmillan, 1938-50) and

the Fitzgerald *Washington* (*see* Authorities) numbers thirty-nine.

25. "I only know I turned to neither book or pamphlet while writing it." Letter from Jefferson to James Madison, 1822. Jefferson, *Papers,* Vol. I, p. 332.

26. The original of this, one of the papers sold to the government by Jefferson's grandson, is in the Library of Congress. It is not to be confused with *the* Declaration of Independence, the final draft, the parchment copy signed by fifty-six delegates to Congress. That is enshrined in the National Archives Building. The reader will find at the back of this book a copy of this final draft, which can be used for purposes of comparison with the Rough Draft printed here.

27. Plumb, *The First Four Georges,* pp. 84-5. Thackeray too, in *The Four Georges,* recites this scene. They both had it from Lord Hervey's *Memoirs.*

28. By his grandson and biographer, Charles Francis Adams.

29. He was placed under what we would now call house arrest, and subsequently was shipped to Connecticut, that stony state which seems to have served as a sort of wartime Siberia; and there, impotent, he remained for the duration. Van Doren, *Benjamin Franklin,* pp. 549-64; Morse, *Benjamin Franklin,* p. 85; Russell, *Benjamin Franklin,* pp. 250-51.

30. He had 7,389 present and fit for duty, plus 365 members of a regiment of artillery, according to his June 28 report to Congress. *Writings,* Vol. V, pp. 190-91.

31. In fact the siege, a fiasco, already had been lifted, but word of this had not yet reached Philadelphia.

32. *Journals,* Vol. IV, pp. 391, 508.

33. Six and two-thirds dollars a month, which when fixed sums had been taken out came to five dollars even. This was the pay for a private. A British private got four shillings sixpence—when he got it. The British, perhaps because they had been in the business longer, had many more methods of impounding parts of a private's wage. The biggest difference between the two, however, was that the Britisher was paid in

hard cash, the Continental in paper money that already had started to plunge and soon was to be worth almost nothing, originating the phrase "not worth a continental." The British helped in this process by printing millions of dollars worth of counterfeit money on board frigates that operated offshore: they had brought along printing presses with this ruse in mind. Hatch, *Administration of the American Revolutionary Army,* p. 71. Even while the delegates to the Continental Congress were debating independence, in lower New York Bay a press aboard H.M.S. *Phoenix,* 44 guns, was turning out $30 bills by the bale. This was the first time that Gresham's Law was made to work as a weapon of war. It was to be by no means the last. In World War II the Germans at one time were manufacturing £5, £10, and £20 Bank of England notes at the rate of 1,800 an hour. Scott, *Counterfeiting in Colonial America,* pp. 12, 253. It should be noted that although pounds and shillings always had been the official currency in the American colonies, the Spanish milled dollar, by reason of the trade with the West Indies, was much more convenient, and for all intents and purposes it had been the colonial standard of computation for some time before Congress formally made it so. This was a silver eight-real piece, though they were sometimes called eight-pieces or (as by Long John Silver's parrot) pieces-of-eight.

34. He appointed Brigadier General Hugh Mercer, an energetic officer, who, however, could do little with what he had here. Washington extended the jurisdiction of the commissary-general, Joseph Trumbull of Connecticut, mercantile son of stout old Governor Jonathan Trumbull, the patriot. The Flying Camp idea, like the Minute Men of Massachusetts and the later Pony Express, had an invigorating name but never amounted to much. July 26 Mercer was reporting to Washington that fewer than 3,000 of the authorized 10,000 militiamen from out of state had so far arrived. *Writings,* Vol. V, p. 344. Desertions were exceedingly heavy. *Writings,* Vol. V, p. 428. Soon, when the British had taken New York and dug themselves in, giving Washington a chance to mass his men in northern New Jersey, the need for the Flying Camp evaporated.

General Mercer was killed in the battle of Princeton. Mercer County, New Jersey, is named after him. Freeman, *George Washington*, Vol. IV, *passim*.

35. The figures look strange today. A British regiment in 1776, on paper, was made up of 35 officers, 32 N.C.O.'s, and 390 men, a total of 457, but few were up to full strength, and virtually all carried on their lists the names of twenty or more "contingent" soldiers who in truth were nonexistent, this being an accepted form of payroll padding. Three hundred and fifty to four hundred is a better figure to use for an average. French, *The First Year*, pp. 553-56; Ward, *War of the Revolution*, Vol. I, Chap. 3; Trevelyan, *American Revolution*, Vol. 2, Chap. XVIII; Curtis, *British Army in the American Revolution*, pp. 1-3.

36. Many did desert, but not so many as might have been expected; and this was believed to be due in part to the language barrier—for British commanders were careful to keep the Hessians away from any part of the colonies, such as the Pennsylvania hinterland, where there might be German-speaking residents—and in part to the truly appalling punishments, even for that time and among that people. Of course not all the "Hessians" were Hessian, but this seemed the easiest thing to call them. Of about 17,000 Germans landed on Staten Island almost one-quarter were Brunswickers, and there were also a few men from Waldeck. Throughout the rest of the war the number was kept close to 20,000 through replacements. The breakdown: Hesse-Cassel 16,992, Hesse-Hanau 2,422, Brunswick 5,723, Anspach-Bayreuth 2,353, Waldeck 1,125, Anhalt-Zerbst 1,160, total 29,875. Lowell, *Hessians in the Revolutionary War*, *passim*.

37. All fears were fully justified. This was the largest army England ever had sent from her shores: there were to be 32,000 fully armed and equipped soldiers in that Staten Island camp (near the Narrows) within a few days, plus marines, and many thousands more of sailors were available. Though it did not make so brave a show, having come in bits and pieces, from Charleston, from Halifax, from several ports in England and

Ireland, and though it largely lacked banners, this fleet indeed was by any standard a greater one than the Invincible Armada —almost twice as many men, more than twice as many vessels. Mahan, *Navies in the War of American Independence,* pp. 38-9; Anderson, *Command of the Howe Brothers,* pp. 68-9; Ward, *War of the Revolution,* Vol. I, pp. 208-10; Ritcheson, *British Politics and the American Revolution,* pp. 197-98; Fortescue, *The Empire and the Army,* pp. 116-17.

38. Note the singular. Pennsylvania and Delaware were separate colonies, but they had once been one, under the same charter and the same governor; Pennsylvanians, and especially Philadelphians—Charles Thompson was a Philadelphian—still thought of Delaware as "the lower counties."

39. Adam, *Clans, Septs and Regiments,* pp. 271-321, 328-39.

40. Letter to Joseph Reed. Oberholtzer, *Robert Morris,* pp. 20-1.

41. "Graphology is one of these pseudo-sciences (along with phrenology, physiognomy, astrology, and numerology). It undertakes to determine the varied qualities and attributes of human personality, and even of human character, from handwriting alone. If it could really do what it undertakes to do graphology would in many cases be of great assistance in determining the authenticity or the authorship of disputed handwriting." Osborn, *Questioned Documents,* p. 435.

42. Trumbull, *Autobiography,* pp. 150-1.

43. The latter class is not as large as its members sometimes think, according to L. G. Pine, editor of *Burke's Peerage* and author of the amusing and instructive *They Came with the Conqueror.*

44. Malone, *Declaration of Independence,* pp. 240-41. Another Presbyterian divine, the Rev. John Joachim Zubly from Savannah, Georgia, had been a member of the Congress before the election of Witherspoon. He came from Switzerland and spoke with a heavy German accent; he was the only member of the Congress who had been born outside the British Empire, and he was not a Signer. He resigned at the end of 1775 when Congress got too radical for him. Meigs, *The Violent Men,*

p. 20; Burnett, *The Continental Congress,* pp. 103-4; Montross, *The Reluctant Rebels,* pp. 94, 130, 252. Dr. Witherspoon is remembered by grammarians as the first purist on this side of the sea. He it was, indeed, who coined the very word "Americanism," which he defined as "an use of phrases or terms, or a construction of sentences, even among people of rank and education, different from the use of the same terms or phrases, or the construction of similar sentences in Great Britain. . . . The word *Americanism,* which I have coined for the purpose, is exactly similar in its formation and significance to the word *Scotticism."* Of the twelve expressions he took the trouble to list as examples, deploring all of them, only one, "mad" for "angry," today still seems unfortunate. Mathews, *The Beginnings of American English,* pp. 13-30; Mencken, *The American Language,* 4th ed., pp. 4-7. Yet Witherspoon was unwavering —and outspoken—in his support of independence: he was one of the "violent men."

45. *New York Times,* June 2, 1957. For a description of the duel see Stevens, *Pistols at Ten Paces,* p. 23.

46. The best description of all this is contained in Mearns' *The Story of a Parchment. See* Authorities.

47. Brown, *Rufus Choate,* p. 326.

48. *The Middle Span,* p. 169.

49. *North American Review,* September 1907. Address by Woodrow Wilson at Jamestown Exposition, Norfolk, Virginia, July 4, 1907, on the occasion of the organization of the Descendants of the Signers of the Declaration of Independence. At that time he was president of Princeton.

*Text of the Declaration of Independence**
IN CONGRESS, JULY 4, 1776.
THE UNANIMOUS DECLARATION OF THE THIRTEEN UNITED STATES OF AMERICA,

WHEN in the Course of human events, it becomes necessary for one people to dissolve the political bands which have connected them with another, and to assume among the powers of the earth, the separate and equal station to which the Laws of Nature and of Nature's God entitle them, a decent respect to the opinions of mankind requires that they should declare the causes which impel them to the separation.——We hold these truths to be self-evident, that all men are created equal, that they are endowed by their Creator with certain unalienable Rights, that among these are Life, Liberty and the pursuit of Happiness.——That to secure these rights, Governments are instituted among Men, deriving their just powers from the consent of the governed, ——That whenever any Form of Government becomes destructive of these ends, it is the Right of the People to alter or to abolish it, and to institute new Government, laying its foundation on such principles and organizing its powers in such form, as to them shall seem most likely to effect their Safety and Happiness. Prudence, indeed, will dictate that Governments long established should not be changed for light and transient causes; and accordingly all experience hath shewn, that mankind are more disposed to suffer, while evils are sufferable, than to right themselves by abolishing the forms to which they are accustomed. But when a long train of abuses and usurpations, pursuing invariably the same Object evinces a design to reduce them under absolute Despotism, it is their right, it is their duty, to throw off such Government, and to provide new Guards for their future security.——Such has been the patient sufferance of these Colonies; and such is now the necessity which constrains them to alter their former Systems of Government. The history of the present King of Great Britain is a history of repeated injuries and usurpations, all having in direct object the establishment of an absolute Tyranny over these States. To prove this, let Facts be submitted to a candid world.——He has refused his Assent to Laws, the most wholesome and necessary for the public good.——He has forbidden his Governors to pass Laws of immediate and pressing importance, unless suspended in their operation till his Assent should be obtained; and when so suspended, he has utterly neglected to attend to them.——He has refused to pass other Laws for the accommodation of large districts of people, unless these people would relinquish the right of Representation in the Legislature, a right inestimable to them and formidable to tyrants only.—— He has called together legislative bodies at places unusual, uncomfortable, and distant from the depository of their public Records, for the sole purpose of fatiguing them into compliance with his measures.——He has dissolved Representative Houses repeatedly, for opposing with manly firmness his invasions on the rights of the people.——He has refused for a long time, after such dissolutions, to cause others to be elected; whereby the Legislative powers, incapable of Annihilation, have returned to the People at large for their exercise; the State remaining in the mean time exposed to all the dangers of invasion from without, and convulsions within.——He has endeavoured to prevent the population of these States; for that purpose obstructing the Laws for Naturalization of Foreigners; refusing to pass others to encourage their migrations hither, and raising the conditions of new Appropriations of Lands.——He has obstructed the Administration of Justice, by refusing his Assent to Laws for establishing Judiciary powers.——He has made Judges dependent on his Will alone, for the tenure of their offices, and the amount and payment of their salaries.——He has erected a multitude of New Offices, and sent hither swarms of Officers to harass our people, and eat out their substance.——He

*This text follows exactly the spelling and punctuation of the original document.

has kept among us, in times of peace, Standing Armies without the Consent of our legislatures.——He has affected to render the Military independent of and superior to the Civil power.——He has combined with others to subject us to a jurisdiction foreign to our constitution, and unacknowledged by our laws; giving his Assent to their Acts of pretended Legislation: —For quartering large bodies of armed troops among us:—For protecting them, by a mock Trial, from punishment for any Murders which they should commit on the Inhabitants of these States:—For cutting off our Trade with all parts of the world:—For imposing Taxes on us without our Consent:—For depriving us in many cases, of the benefits of Trial by Jury:—For transporting us beyond Seas to be tried for pretended offences:—For abolishing the free System of English Laws in a neighbouring Province, establishing therein an Arbitrary government, and enlarging its Boundaries so as to render it at once an example and fit instrument for introducing the same absolute rule into these Colonies:——For taking away our Charters, abolishing our most valuable Laws, and altering fundamentally the Forms of our Governments:—For suspending our own Legislatures and declaring themselves invested with power to legislate for us in all cases whatsoever.—He has abdicated Government here, by declaring us out of his Protection and waging War against us.——He has plundered our seas, ravaged our Coasts, burnt our towns, and destroyed the lives of our people.——He is at this time transporting large Armies of foreign Mercenaries to compleat the works of death, desolation and tyranny, already begun with circumstances of Cruelty & perfidy scarcely paralleled in the most barbarous ages, and totally unworthy the Head of a civilized nation.—— He has constrained our fellow Citizens taken Captive on the high Seas to bear Arms against their Country, to become the executioners of their friends and Brethren, or to fall themselves by their Hands.—— He has excited domestic insurrections amongst us, and has endeavoured to bring on the inhabitants of our frontiers, the merciless Indian Savages, whose known rule of warfare, is an undistinguished destruction of all ages, sexes and conditions. In every stage of these Oppressions We have Petitioned for Redress in the most humble terms: Our repeated Petitions have been answered only by repeated injury. A Prince, whose character is thus marked by every act which may define a Tyrant, is unfit to be the ruler of a free people. Nor have We been wanting in attentions to our Brittish brethren. We have warned them from time to time of attempts by their legislature to extend an unwarrantable jurisdiction over us. We have reminded them of the circumstances of our emigration and settlement here. We have appealed to their native justice and magnanimity, and we have conjured them by the ties of our common kindred to disavow these usurpations, which, would inevitably interrupt our connections and correspondence They too have been deaf to the voice of justice and of consanguinity. We must, therefore, acquiesce in the necessity, which denounces our Separation, and hold them, as we hold the rest of mankind, Enemies in War, in Peace Friends.—

WE, THEREFORE, the Representatives of the united States of America, in General Congress, Assembled, appealing to the Supreme Judge of the world for the rectitude of our intentions, do, in the Name, and by Authority of the good People of these Colonies, solemnly publish and declare, That these United Colonies are, and of Right ought to be FREE AND INDEPENDENT STATES; that they are Absolved from all Allegiance to the British Crown, and that all political connection between them and the State of Great Britain, is and ought to be totally dissolved; and that as Free and Independent States, they have full Power to levy War, conclude Peace, contract Alliances, establish Commerce, and to do all other Acts and Things which Independent States may of right do.——And for the support of this Declaration, with a firm reliance on the protection of divine Providence, we mutually pledge to each other our Lives, our Fortunes and our sacred Honor.

Authorities

Authorities

THIS BOOK was compiled from other books. No original research was attempted, and there is no claim that some dusty, barely legible letter retrieved from an old-time attic has been used to "shed new light" on so majestic a subject.

In many cases, perhaps most, the source is obvious and needs no note, except, conceivably, for purposes of supplement.

These five works, not often acknowledged, are the pillars upon which the tale most heavily rests:

Journals of the Continental Congress 1774-1789, ed. by WORTHINGTON CHAUNCEY FORD. Washington: Government Printing Office, 1904.

Letters of Members of the Continental Congress, ed. by EDMUND C. BURNETT, 8 vols. Washington, D. C.: Carnegie Institute of Washington, 1921-36.

The Papers of Thomas Jefferson, ed. by JULIAN P. BOYD, 13 vols. Princeton, N. J.: Princeton University Press, 1950.

The Works of John Adams, with Life, ed. by CHARLES FRANCIS ADAMS, 10 vols. Boston: Little, Brown & Co., 1850-56.

The Writings of George Washington, from the Original Manuscript Courses, 1745-1799, ed. by JOHN C. FITZPATRICK, 39 vols. Washington, D. C.: U. S. Government Printing Office, 1931-44.

The principal works on the Declaration itself and on the Signers are listed below. Of these I found Malone the most readable, Becker the most thoughtful, and Hazleton (though rough going) the most thorough.

BECKER, CARL. *The Declaration of Independence: A Study in the History of Political Ideas.* New York: Peter Smith, 1933.

BOYD, JULIAN. *The Declaration of Independence: The Evolution of the Text.* Princeton, N. J.: Princeton University Press, 1943.

BROTHERHEAD, WILLIAM. *The Book of the Signers.* Philadelphia: W. Brotherhead, 1861.

DANA, W. F. "The Declaration of Independence as Justification for Revolution," *Harvard Law Review,* XIII (January, 1900) pp. 319-43.

DARLING, ARTHUR B. *A Historical Introduction to the Declaration of Independence.* New Haven, Conn.: Quinnipack Press, Inc., 1932.

DUMBAULD, EDWARD. *The Declaration of Independence and What It Means Today*. Norman, Olka.: University of Oklahoma Press, 1950.

FRIEDENWALD, HERBERT. *The Declaration of Independence: An Interpretation and an Analysis*. New York: The Macmillan Company, 1904.

GOODRICH, Rev. CHARLES AUGUSTUS. *Lives of the Signers to the Declaration of Independence*. New York: W. Reed & Co., 1829.

HAZELTON, JOHN H. *The Declaration of Independence: Its History*. New York: Dodd, Mead & Co., 1906.

LEFFMAN, HENRY. "The Real Declaration of Independence," *Pennsylvania Magazine of History and Biography*, XLVII pp. 261-97.

LOSSING, JOHN BENSON. *Biographical Sketches of the Signers of the Declaration of Independence*. New York: G. F. Cooledge and Bro., 1848.

MALONE, DUMAS. *The Story of the Declaration of Independence*. New York: Oxford University Press, 1954.

MCARTHUR, ANNABEL DOUGLAS. *See* SINCLAIR.

MCGEE, DOROTHY HORTON. *Famous Signers of the Declaration*. New York: Dodd, Mead & Co., 1955.

MEARNS, DAVID C. *The Declaration of Independence: The Story of a Parchment*. Washington, D. C.: Library of Congress, 1950.

SANDERSON, JOHN. *Biography of the Signers to the Declaration of Independence*, 7 vols. Philadelphia: R. W. Pomeroy, 1820-27.

SINCLAIR, MERLE, and MCARTHUR, ANNABEL DOUGLAS. *They Signed for Us*. New York: Duell, Sloan & Pearce, 1957.

THOMPSON, CHARLES ORRIN FREEMAN. *A History of the Declaration of Independence*. Bristol, R. I.: published by the author, 1947.

General histories that have been useful include:

ANDERSON, TROYER STEELE. *The Command of the Howe Brothers During the American Revolution*. New York and London: Oxford University Press, 1936.

BECKER, CARL. *The Eve of the Revolution: a Chronicle of the Breach with England*. New Haven: Yale University Press, 1918.

BURNETT, EDMUND C. *The Continental Congress*. New York: The Macmillan Company, 1941.

CURTIS, E. E. *The British Army in the American Revolution*. New Haven: Yale University Press, 1926.

DRAKE, FRANCIS S., ed. *Tea Leaves: Being a Collection of Letters and Documents relating to the Shipment of Tea to the American Colonies in the Year 1773 by the East India Tea Company*. Boston: A. O. Crane, 1884.

ELLIS, GEORGE EDWARD. *The Sentiment of Independence: Its Growth and Consummation. (Narrative and Critical History of America*, ed. Justin Winsor, Vol. 6.) Boston: Houghton Mifflin Co., 1888.

FISHER, SYDNEY GEORGE. *The Struggle for American Independence*, 2 vols. Philadelphia: J. B. Lippincott Co., 1908.

FISK, JOHN. *The American Revolution*, 2 vols. Boston & New York: Houghton Mifflin Co., 1891.

FRENCH, ALLEN. *The First Year of the American Revolution*. Boston: Houghton Mifflin Co., 1934.

FROTHINGHAM, RICHARD. *The Rise of the Republic of the United States*, 10th ed. Boston: Little, Brown & Co., 1910.

GIPSON, LAWRENCE HENRY. *The Coming of the American Revolution, 1763-1775*. New York: Harper & Brothers, 1954.

HOWARD, GEORGE ELLIOTT. *Preliminaries of the American Revolution*. New York: Harper & Brothers, 1905.

LECKY, W. E. H. *History of England in the Eighteenth Century*, 8 vols. London: Longmans, Green & Co., 1878-90.

MAHAN, A. T. *The Major Operations of the Navies in the War of American Independence*. London: Sampson Low, Marston & Company, 1913.

MEIGS, CORNELIA. *The Violent Men: a Study of the Human Relations in the First American Congress*. New York: The Macmillan Company, 1949.

MILLER, JOHN C. *Origins of the American Revolution*. Boston: Little, Brown & Co., 1943.

MONTROSS, LYNN. *Rag, Tag and Bobtail: The Story of the Continental Army*. New York: Harper & Brothers, 1952.

_____. *The Reluctant Rebels: The Story of the Continental Congress*. New York: Harper & Brothers, 1950.

MORRIS, RICHARD B., editor. *The Era of the American Revolution*. New York: Columbia University Press, 1939.

PRESTON, JOHN HYDE. *Revolution: 1776*. New York: Harcourt, Brace & Co., 1933.

ROSSITER, CLINTON. *Seedtime of the Republic: The Origin of the American Tradition of Political Liberty*. New York: Harcourt, Brace & Co., 1953.

SCHLESINGER, ARTHUR MEIER. *The Colonial Merchants and the American Revolution*. New York: The Facsimile Library, Inc., 1939.

SCHOULER, JAMES. *Americans of 1776*. New York: Dodd, Mead & Co., 1906.

TREVELYAN, GEORGE OTTO. *The American Revolution*, 6 vols. London: Longmans, Green & Co., 1905.

TYLER, MOSES COIT. *The Literary History of the American Revolution*, 2 vols. New York: G. P. Putnam's Sons, 1897.

WARD, CHRISTOPHER. *The War of the Revolution*, 2 vols. New York: The Macmillan Company, 1952.

WINSOR, JUSTIN, ed. *The Memorial History of Boston, 1630-1880*, 4 vols. Boston: J. R. Osgood and Company, 1880-81.

_____. *Narrative and Critical History of America*, Vol. 6. Boston: Houghton Mifflin Co., 1887.

Among other books mentioned or quoted in the text are these:

ADAM, FRANK. *The Clans, Septs and Regiments of the Scottish Highlands*. Edinburgh and London: W. & A. K. Johnston, Ltd., 1908.

ADAMS, CHARLES FRANCIS, editor. *Familiar Letters of John Adams and His Wife Abigail Adams, during the Revolution*. New York: Hurd and Houghton, 1876.

ADAMS, JAMES TRUSLOW. *The Adams Family*. Boston: Little, Brown & Co., 1930.

ALEXANDER, EDWARD P. *A Revolutionary Conservative: James Duane of New York*. New York: Columbia University Press, 1938.

AUSTIN, JAMES TRECOTHICK. *The Life of Elbridge Gerry, with Contemporary Letters to the Close of the American Revolution*, 2 vols. Boston: Wealls and Lilly, 1828-29.

BEARDSLEY, EBEN EDWARDS. *Life and Correspondence of the Right Reverend Samuel Seabury, D.D.*, 2d edition. Boston: Houghton Mifflin Co., 1881.

BOWEN, CATHERINE DRINKER. *John Adams and the American Revolution*. Boston: Little, Brown & Co., 1950.

BROWN, SAMUEL GILMAN. *The Life of Rufus Choate*, 6th edition. Boston: Little Brown & Co., 1898.

BRUNHOUSE, ROBERT L. *The Counter-Revolution in Pennsylvania, 1776-1790*. Harrisburg, Pa.: Pennsylvania Historical Commission, 1942.

DAVIDSON, PHILIP. *Propaganda and the American Revolution, 1763-1783*. Chapel Hill: University of North Carolina Press, 1941.

DOWNS, ROBERT B. *Books That Changed the World*. Chicago: American Library Association, 1956.

FORBES, ESTHER. *Paul Revere and the World He Lived In*. Boston: Houghton Mifflin Company, 1942.

FORTESCUE, SIR JOHN WILLIAM. *The Empire and the Army*. London: Cassell and Co., Ltd., 1928.

FRANKLIN, BENJAMIN. *Autobiographical Writings*, ed. by Carl van Doren. New York: The Viking Press, 1945.

FREEMAN, DOUGLAS SOUTHALL, *George Washington: a Biography*, 6 vols., New York, Charles Scribner's Sons, 1948-54.

GUEDALLA, PHILIP. *Independence Day*. London, John Murray, 1926.

HARLEY, L. R. *Life of Charles Thompson*. Philadelphia: Jacobs, 1900.

HATCH, LOUIS CLINTON. *The Administration of the American Revolutionary Army*. New York: Longmans, Green & Co., Inc., 1904.

HOSMER, J. K. *Samuel Adams*. Boston: Houghton Mifflin Co., 1885.

IRVING, WASHINGTON. *The Life of Washington*, 3 vols. New York: Frank F. Lovell Company, 1856.

JENNINGS, JOHN. *Boston: Cradle of Liberty*. New York: Doubleday & Co., 1947.

KNOLLENBERG, BERNHARD. *Washington and the Revolution: a Reappraisal*. New York: The Macmillan Company, 1940.

LITTLE, SHELBY. *George Washington*. New York: Minton Balch & Company, 1929.

LONG, J. C. *Mr. Pitt and America's Birthright*. New York: Frederick A. Stokes, Inc., 1940.

LOWELL, EDWARD J. *The Hessians and the Other German Auxiliaries of Great Britain in the Revolutionary War*. New York: Harper & Brothers, 1884.

MALONE, DUMAS. *Jefferson the Virginian*. Boston: Little, Brown & Co., 1948.

MANROSS, WILLIAM WILSON. *A History of the American Episcopal Church*. New York and Milwaukee: Morehouse Publishing Co., 1935.

MATHEWS, M. M. *The Beginnings of American English*. Chicago: University of Chicago Press, 1931.

MENCKEN, HENRY LOUIS. *The American Language*, 3d ed. New York: Alfred A. Knopf, Inc., 1923.

MILLER, JOHN C. *Sam Adams.* Boston: Little, Brown & Co., 1936.
MILLER, PERRY. *The New England Mind.* New York: The Macmillan Company, 1939.
MORSE, JOHN T., JR. *Benjamin Franklin.* Boston: Houghton Mifflin Company, 1891.
――――――. *John Adams.* Boston: Houghton Mifflin Company, 1899.
MOTT, FRANK LUTHER. *Golden Multitudes: The Story of Best Sellers in the United States.* New York: The Macmillan Company, 1947.
OBERHOLTZER, ELLIS PAXSON. *Robert Morris: Patriot and Financier.* New York: The Macmillan Company, 1903.
OSBORN, ALBERT S. *Questioned Documents*, 2d ed. Albany, N. Y.: Boyd Printing Company, 1929.
PAINE, THOMAS. *See* WHEELER.
PARES, RICHARD. *King George III and the Politicians.* New York: Clarendon Press (Oxford), 1953.
PINE, L. G. *They Came with the Conqueror: a Study of the Descendants of the Normans.* New York: G. P. Putnam's Sons, 1957.
PLUMB, J. H. *The First Four Georges.* New York: The Macmillan Company, 1957.
RILEY, EDWARD M. *History of the Independence Hall Group* (reprinted from "Historical Philadelphia, From the Founding until the Early Nineteenth Century," Transactions of the American Philosophical Society, Vol. 43, Part I, March, 1953). Philadelphia.
RITCHESON, CHARLES R. *British Politics and the American Revolution.* Norman, Okla.: University of Oklahoma Press, 1954.
ROSEWATER, VICTOR. *The Liberty Bell: Its History and Significance.* New York: D. Appleton & Co., 1926.
ROWLAND, KATE MASON. *The Life of Charles Carroll of Carrollton, 1737-1832*, 2 vols. New York and London: G. P. Putnam's Sons, 1899.
RUSSELL, PHILLIPS. *Benjamin Franklin: The First Civilized American.* New York: Brentano's, 1927.
――――――. *Jefferson: Champion of the Free Mind.* New York: Dodd, Mead & Co., 1956.
SANTAYANA, GEORGE. *The Middle Span.* New York: Charles Scribner's Sons, 1945.
SCHACHNER, NATHAN. *Thomas Jefferson: a Biography*, 2 vols. New York: Appleton-Century-Crofts, Inc., 1951.
SCOTT, KENNETH. *Counterfeiting in Colonial America.* New York: Oxford University Press, 1957.
SEABURY, REV. SAMUEL. *Letters of a Westchester Farmer (1774-1775)*, edited and with an introduction by Clarence H. Vance; published for Westchester County by the Westchester County Historical Society. White Plains, N. Y., 1930.
STEVENS, WILLIAM OLIVER. *Pistols at Ten Paces: The Story of the Code of Honor in America.* Boston: Houghton Mifflin Company, 1940.
STILLE, CHARLES J. *The Life and Times of John Dickinson, 1732-1808.* Philadelphia: Historical Society of Pennsylvania, 1891.

SUTHERLAND, STELLA H. *Population Distribution in Colonial America.* New York: Columbia University Press, 1956.

SWEET, WILLIAM WARREN. *Religion in Colonial America.* New York: Charles Scribner's Sons, 1942.

TAYLOR, EMERSON. *Paul Revere.* New York: Edward Valentine Mitchell and Dodd, Mead & Company, 1930.

TRUMBULL, JOHN. *Autobiography, Reminiscences and Letters, from 1756 to 1841.* New Haven, Conn.: B. L. Hamlen, 1841.

TRUMBULL, JONATHAN. *Jonathan Trumbull, Governor of Connecticut, 1769-1784.* Boston: Little, Brown & Company, 1919.

TYLER, MOSES COIT. *Patrick Henry.* Boston: Houghton Mifflin Company, 1898.

VANCE. *See* SEABURY.

VAN DOREN, CARL. *Benjamin Franklin.* New York: The Viking Press, 1938.

VAN TYME, CHARLES HALSTEAD. *The Loyalists in the American Revolution.* New York: The Macmillan Company, 1902.

WALSH, CORREA MOYLAN. *The Political Science of John Adams.* New York: G. P. Putnam's Sons, 1915.

WHEELER, DANIEL EDWIN, ed. *Life and Writings of Thomas Paine,* 10 vols. New York: Vincent Parke and Company, 1915.

Index

Act of Union, 90
Adams, Abigail, 22, 72, 74
Adams, Charles Francis, 72, n.28
Adams, John, 22-4, 30-1, 40, 49, 56, 58-9, 61, 68-9, 72, 74, 79, 84, 88, 95, 102, 110-1, 123-4
Adams, John Quincy, 113
Adams, Samuel, 11-12, 15-18, 23, 28, 71, 102, 105, 110, n.9
Allen, Andrew, 49
Allen, Ethan, 13
Arnold, Gen. Benedict, 13, 21, 33
American Philosophical Society, 56, 98
Amherst, Lord Jeffrey, 20
Anspach, Caroline of, 71
Auchmuty, Samuel, 47
Auxiliaries, see Hessians
Barré, Isaac, 18, 19
Bartlett, Josiah, 25, 92, 102
Biddle, Edward, 49
Bill of Rights, 120
Bonvouloir, Achard de, 75
Boucher, Jonathan, 47
Braddock, Gen. Edward, 18
Braxton, Carter, 6, 46, 59, 103, 109
Burgoyne, Gen. John, 33, 78, 81
Burke, Edmund, 19
Campbell, Lt. Col., 54
Carleton, Gen. Guy, 33
Carpenter's Hall, 28, 63
Carroll, Charles of Annapolis, 109
Carroll, Charles of Carrollton, 17, 97, 103, 108, 109, n.20
Carroll, Rev. John, 97, 108
Catherine the Great, of Russia, 80
Caulkers' Club, 15, n.6
Chandler, Thomas Bradbury, 47
Charles III of Spain, 50
Chase, Samuel, 31, 48, 103, 104
Chatham, Lord, see Pitt
Chesterfield, Lord, 91
Choate, Rufus, 122, n.47
Clark, Abraham, 29, 103, 105, 110
Cleveland, Grover, 111
Clinton, Gen. Henry, 79
Clymer, George, 103
Colby, Bainbridge, 116
Common Sense, 36, 37, 38, 68, n.13
Conway, Lord, 21, n.8
Coolidge, Calvin, 117
Cooper, Miles, 47
Cushing, Thomas, 32
Deane, Silas, 50
Declaration of Right, 120
Delanceys, the, 27
Depeysters, the, 27

149

Dickinson, John, 22-4, 43-5, 48-9, 51, 55, 57, 93, 104
Duane, James, 39, 40, 48
Dunlap, John, 97-8, 105
Effingham, Lord, 20
Fairhill, 43, 104
Floyd, William, 102, 110
Flying Camp, the, 78-80, n.34
Franklin, Benjamin, 5, 19, 29, 42-3, 49, 55, 58-9, 61, 74-5, 77-8, 83-5, 94-5, 97, 103, 107, 110-1
Franklin, William, 77-8, n.29
Frederick the Great, 80
Gadsden, Christopher, 26
Gage, Gen. Thomas, 13, 20
Galloway, Joseph, 15, 16, 44, n.7
Garrison, John, 95
Gates, Gen. Horatio, 79
George I of Great Britain, 21, 34, 71
George II of Great Britain, 34, 71
George III of Great Britain, 20-4, 31-4, 36, 38-9, 44, 47, 64-8, 71, 81, 84, 86, 90, 98-9, 124-5
Gerry, Albridge, 32, 43, 102, 104, 110, n.12
Graaf, Frederic, 5, 69
Greene, Gen. Nathaniel, 54
Gwinnet, Button, 93, 103, 106, 108
Hall, Lyman, 79, 93, 103, 106, 110
Hamilton, Alexander, 102, n.19
Hancock, John, 13, 17, 41-3, 51, 58-9, 83, 93, 99-101, 105, 110
Harding, Warren Gamaliel, 116-7
Harrison, Benjamin, 22, 41-3, 51, 58, 79, 83, 103, 110-1
Harrison, President Benjamin, 110
Harrison, William Henry, 110-1
Hart, John, 29, 102, 109
Hay, John, 116
Henry, Patrick, 26, 45, 59, 75, 92, 102
Hertford, Duke of, 21
Hessians, the, 11, 33, 80, 81, n.36, n.37
Hewes, Joseph, 48, 79, 93, 103, 108, 110
Hichborne, Benjamin, 21-3
Hooker, Richard, 120
Hooper, William, 110
Hopkins, Stephen, 79, 102, 106, 107
Hopkinson, Francis, 29, 103, 106
Howe, Emmanuel, 2nd viscount, 21
Howe, George, 3rd viscount, 21
Howe, Adm. Richard, 21, 28, 75, 78, 94
Howe, Gen. William, 10, 11, 21, 28, 33, 54, 78, 94
Hughes, Charles Evans, 116-7
Huntington, Samuel, 110
Humphries, Charles, 49, 55, 58
Inglis, Charles, 47
James II of England, 120
Jay, John, 112
Jefferson, Martha, 87

Index

Jefferson, Thomas, 3, 5, 18, 20, 44, 58-9, 61, 63, 68-9, 71, 74, 77-8, 81, 83-5, 87-8, 90-2, 95, 100-1, 110-2, 120-1, 124-5, n.24, n.25, n.26
Keppel, Lord, 20
Kielmannsegge, Baroness (Countess of Darlington), 21, 71
Lafayette, Marquis de, 118-9
Lee, Francis Lightfoot, 103, 110
Lee, Richard Henry (the signer), 40, 41, 57, 59, 79, 103, 104, 110, 123
Lee, Richard Henry (the grandson), 114
Lee, the family, 18
Letters from a Farmer in Pennsylvania, etc., 44, 45
Littlejohn, Rev. Mr., 113
Livingston, Robert, 48, 58, 59, 79, 104
Livingston, William, 79
Livingston, the family, 17, 27
Locke, John, 120-1
Louis XVI of France, 50
Lynch, Thomas, 107
Lynch, Thomas Jr., 107, 103, 110
MacLeish, Archibald, 117
Magna Carta, 119, 120
Mary, Queen of England, 120
Mason, George, of Gunsden Hall, 63, 123
Massachusetts Gazette, 23
Matlack, Timothy, 100
McIntosh, Brig. Lachlan, 108
McKean, Thomas, 29, 42, 51, 56, 88, 103, 104, 105
Mencken, Henry L., 122, n.44
Mercer, Gen. Hugh, 34
Merchant, George, 80
Middleton, Arthur, 103
Mifflin, Brig. Thomas, 79
Monroe, James, 113
Montgomery, John, 94-5
Montgomery, Gen. Richard, 33
Morgenthau, Henry, 117
Morris, Robert, 49, 55, 93, 103, 110, n.40
Morton, John, 29, 49, 55, 57, 58, 103, 106, 108, 109
Nelson, Thomas Jr., 8
Nelsons, the, 18
Nixon, John, 98
Paca, William, 48, 103, 106
Paine, Robert Treat, 102, 110
Paine, Thomas, 36-8, 68, n.13
Patterson, Edgar, 113
Penn, Richard, 5
Pennsylvania Evening Post, 123
Pennsylvania Gazette, 80, 123
Peters, Samuel, 47
Philip II of Spain, 38
Pickering, Timothy, 27, n.22
Pitt, William, see Chatham
Poor Richard's Almanack, 77
Prohibitory Act, 34, 36

Putnam, Herbert, 117
Randall, Ben, 61
Randolph, Peyton, 59, 100
Read, George, 29, 79, 103, 104
Reed, Joseph, n.40
Rodney, Caesar, 29, 42, 51, 54, 56, 57, 103, 110
Rogers, William B., 116
Rough Draft, 61-8
Rush, Dr. Benjamin, 89, 92, 103, 106
Rutledge, Edward, 30, 41, 49, 51, 103, 107
Rutledge, John, 30
Santayana, George, 122, n.48
Schuyler, Gen. Philip, 21
Schuylers, the, 27
Schulenburg, Ehrengard von, Duchess of Kendal, 71
Seabury, the Rev. Samuel, 47, n.19
Sherman, Roger, 58, 59, 79, 102
Smith, James, 103, 108, 110
Smith, Sydney, 44
Stamp Act, 8, 19, 44
State House, Philadelphia, 6-9, 12, 17, 29, 47, 51, 54-6, 63, 74, 77, 87, 93, 98, 113
Stockton, Richard, 29, 89, 102
Stone, Thomas, 48, 103
Sullivan, Gen. John, 21, 26
Taylor, George, 103, 106
Thompson, Charles, 12, 21, 31, 41, 57, 83, 93, 98, 100, 112, n.38
Thornton, Matthew, 79, 102, 104
Townshend Acts, 8
Trumbull, John, 101, n.42
Trumbull, Jonathan, 54, 101, n.34
Van Cortlandts, the, 27
Voltaire, 45, 91
Walton, George, 93, 103, 110
Ward, Gen. Artemas, 54
Warren, James, 22-4
Washington, George, 6, 9, 10, 13, 17, 21, 26, 31, 33, 51, 54, 59, 71, 78-81, 94, 98, 102, 112, 114
Webster, Daniel, 113
Whipple, William, 79, 92, 102, 110
Wilkes, John, 19
William of Orange, 120
William the Conqueror, 37, 101
Williams, William, 102, 110
Willing, Thomas, 49, 55, 58
Wilson, James, 29, 32, 36, 49, 55, 58, 75, 79, 83, 88, 95, 110
Wilson, Woodrow, 116, 123, n.49
Wisner, Henry, 94
Wolcott, Oliver, 102, 110
Wolfe, Gen. James, 18
Witherspoon, the Rev. John, 29, 49, 88, 102, 106, 123, n.44
Wythe, George, 59, 103, 110
Yeates, Jasper, 94

www.ingramcontent.com/pod-product-compliance
Lightning Source LLC
LaVergne TN
LVHW041625070426
835507LV00008B/461